Creator Can You Hear Me:

A collection of 70 prayers to the Creator

Written by

Holden Schroder

Dedicated to

Andrea Schroder

For being a living example of living in the Light of Love and that when hardship knocks to not surrender to the pain but to seek growth and guidance.

In that light may this collection of prayers be an instrument for you to expand and articulate your intentions to the divine creator.

Prayers

1. Prayer of Love
2. Prayer of Gratitude
3. Prayer of the Day
4. Prayer of Forgiveness
5. Prayer of Forgiving Others
6. Prayer of Strength
7. Prayer of Faith
8. Prayer of Understanding
9. Prayer of Freedom
10. Prayer of Expansion
11. Prayer of Purpose
12. Prayer of Power
13. Prayer of Healing
14. Prayer of Fun
15. Prayer for a New Career Path
16. Prayer to Be a Boss
17. Prayer of Creativity
18. Prayer of Happiness
19. Prayer of Health
20. Prayer of Wealth
21. Prayer of Improvement
22. Prayer of Dedication
23. Prayer of Peace
24. Prayer of Evolution
25. Prayer of Humility
26. Prayer of Sharing
27. Prayer of Mercy
28. Prayer of Family
29. Prayer of Leadership
30. Prayer of Adventure
31. Prayer of Excellence
32. Prayer of Courage
33. Prayer of Travel
34. Prayer of Learning
35. Prayer of Attraction
36. Prayer of Balance
37. Prayer of Ridding Vices
38. Prayer of Romance
39. Prayer of Acceptance
40. Prayer of Creation
41. Prayer of Service
42. Prayer of Fulfillment
43. Prayer of Manifestation
44. Prayer of Self-Care

45. Prayer of Intuition
46. Prayer of Confidence
47. Prayer of Generosity
48. Prayer of Empathy
49. Prayer of Honesty
50. Prayer of Wisdom
51. Prayer of Patience
52. Prayer of Integrity
53. Prayer of Productivity
54. Prayer of Accomplishment
55. Prayer of Positivity
56. Prayer of Clarity
57. Prayer of Rest
58. Prayer of Energy
59. Prayer about the Dream Life
60. Prayer about the Dream House
61. Prayer of Action
62. Prayer of Transformation
63. Prayer of Protection
64. Prayer of Focus
65. Prayer to Mother Earth
66. Prayer of Spirituality
67. Prayer of Potential
68. Prayer of Recovering from Illness
69. Prayer of Friendship
70. Prayer of Thanks

Help is given to those that ask for it…

A Prayer of Love

Divine Creator,
I express my pray with a humble heart,
Seeking guidance and solace in matters of love.
You are the embodiment of unconditional love,
The source from which all love flows,
And I ask for your presence and blessings now.

Grant me the wisdom to understand love's true nature,
To see beyond the surface and perceive its depths.
Help me embrace love in all its forms,
From the tenderness of romantic love to the compassion of friendship,
From the bond between parent and child to the love shared among humanity.

Guide me to love fearlessly and authentically,
To let go of judgment and embrace acceptance.
Teach me to see the beauty in every soul,
To recognize the divine spark that resides within each being.

Grant me the strength to forgive,
To let go of past hurts and grievances,
And to open my heart to new possibilities.
Help me cultivate patience and understanding,
To nurture relationships and mend broken bonds.

May I be a vessel of love in this world,
Radiating kindness, compassion, and empathy.
Let me be a source of comfort and support,
Offering a listening ear and a caring heart.

May love be a guiding force in my life,
A beacon of light in times of darkness,
A source of strength in moments of weakness.
Help me to love myself deeply and unconditionally,
So that I may overflow with love for others.

I surrender my heart to the divine flow of love,
Trusting that it will lead me on the path of joy and fulfillment.
Thank you, Divine Creator, for the gift of love,
And for the endless opportunities it brings.

With love and gratitude, I pray,
Amen.

Notes - Personal Prayer

A Prayer for Gratitude

Divine Creator,

I speak now with a heart overflowing with gratitude,
For the countless gifts and miracles that appear in my life.
In this sacred moment, I offer my deepest appreciation,
For the beauty that surrounds me and all the many blessings I receive.

I am grateful for the gift of life itself,
For the breath that fills my lungs and the beating of my heart.
Each day is a precious opportunity to experience the wonders of existence,
And I am humbled by the sheer magnitude of this gift.

I am grateful for the natural world that surrounds me,
For the majestic mountains, the serene oceans, and the vibrant forests.
These manifestations of your divine creation remind me of your limitless power,
And inspire me to connect with the inherent beauty and harmony in all things.

I am grateful for the love and support of my family and friends,
For their presence in my life and the bonds we share.
Their laughter and companionship bring warmth to my soul,
And their unwavering support uplifts me in times of challenge.

I am grateful for the lessons learned through hardships,
For the trials that have shaped me into the person I am today.
In moments of struggle, I have discovered my strength,
And through adversity, I have grown in resilience and wisdom.

I am grateful for the abundance that fills my life,
For the opportunities that come my way and the resources at my disposal.
I recognize the privilege that allows me to fulfill my needs and desires,
And I pledge to use these blessings to make a positive difference in the world.

I am grateful for the power of choice and free will,
For the ability to create my reality and shape my destiny.
With this gift, I commit to living a life of purpose,
To spread love, kindness, and compassion wherever I go.

Divine Creator, I offer my heartfelt gratitude,
For your infinite love, guidance, and divine presence in my life.
Thank you for the blessings bestowed upon me,
And for the miracles yet to unfold.

With a heart full of gratitude, I pray,
Amen.

Notes - Personal Prayer

A Prayer for the Day

Divine Creator,
As the sun rises and a new day begins,
I turn to you in prayer, seeking your guidance and blessings.
May this day be filled with your divine presence,
And may it unfold with grace, purpose, and joy.

Grant me the wisdom to navigate the challenges that may arise,
And the strength to overcome any obstacles in my path.
Help me to embrace the opportunities that come my way,
And to make the most of each moment, living fully and intentionally.

Bless my mind with clarity and focus,
That I may approach my tasks with diligence and enthusiasm.
Guide my thoughts and actions towards goodness,
So that I may contribute to the well-being of others and the world.

Fill my heart with compassion and kindness,
That I may extend love and understanding to all I encounter.
Grant me the ability to forgive and let go of past grievances,
And to foster harmonious relationships built on respect and empathy.

In times of uncertainty, grant me faith and trust,
Knowing that you are always by my side, guiding me forward.
Help me to surrender control and embrace the flow of life,
Finding peace in the midst of change and uncertainty.

As I embark on this day, may I be a beacon of light,
Radiating positivity and uplifting those around me.
May my words be a source of encouragement,
And my actions inspire others to pursue their dreams.
Divine Creator, I express my gratitude for the gift of this day,
For the opportunities it holds and the lessons it brings.

I surrender to your divine plan and purpose,
Trusting that this day is part of a greater tapestry of life.

With a humble heart, I offer this prayer,
And I ask for your blessings throughout this day.
In your sacred name, I pray,
Amen.

Notes - Personal Prayer

A Prayer for Forgiveness

Divine Creator,
I speak to you with a troubled heart,
Seeking your guidance and healing power in the realm of forgiveness.

I acknowledge the weight of my transgressions,
And the pain I may have caused others through my words or actions.
I humbly ask for your forgiveness,
For any harm I have caused knowingly or unknowingly.

Grant me the courage to confront my mistakes,
And the strength to take responsibility for my actions.
I recognize the importance of forgiveness in my own life,
And the liberation it brings to both the giver and receiver.
Help me release any resentment or anger I hold within me,
And replace it with compassion, understanding, and empathy.

Grant me the wisdom to learn from my mistakes,
To grow and evolve into a better version of myself.

Guide me towards self-forgiveness, for I know that healing begins within,
And allow me to extend that same forgiveness to others.
I understand that forgiveness does not mean condoning hurtful behavior,
But rather, it is a transformative act of letting go and moving forward.

Help me to set healthy boundaries and make amends where necessary,
While still holding space for forgiveness and reconciliation.
Grant me the humility to seek forgiveness from those I have wronged,
And the patience to accept their response, whatever it may be.

May my sincere apologies be received with an open heart,
And may the wounds caused by my actions begin to heal.
Divine Creator, I ask for your divine intervention,
To mend broken relationships and restore harmony.
Guide me towards forgiveness, both for myself and others,
So that I may experience the freedom and peace it brings.

I offer gratitude for the opportunity to grow and evolve through forgiveness,
And for the grace and compassion you bestow upon us all.
Thank you for the gift of redemption and second chances,
And for the path of healing and renewal that forgiveness provides.

With a pure heart, I pray for forgiveness,
And I humbly ask for your continued guidance on this journey.
In your merciful name, I pray,
Amen.

Notes - Personal Prayer

A Prayer About Forgiving Others

Divine Creator
I speak now seeking your guidance and grace as I embark on this sacred journey.
I recognize that forgiveness is a divine act,
And I come before you now, ready to release the burdens of resentment and anger.

Grant me the strength to let go of the pain caused by others,
To release the grip of bitterness that holds me captive.
Help me to understand that forgiveness is not a sign of weakness,
But a profound act of courage and liberation.

In moments of hurt and betrayal, guide me to see the humanity in others,
To recognize that they too may be wounded or struggling.
Help me to cultivate empathy and compassion,
So that I may understand their actions and find a path towards forgiveness.

Divine Creator, I surrender my desire for revenge or retribution,
And instead, I choose the path of forgiveness and healing.
Grant me the wisdom to separate the actions from the person,
To acknowledge the pain they caused while holding space for their potential for change and growth.

I release the heavy burden of grudges and resentments,
Knowing that they only weigh down my spirit and hinder my own growth.
Grant me the grace to forgive, not only for the sake of others,
But for my own peace of mind and emotional well-being.

Help me to find the words to express my forgiveness,
Whether through a heartfelt conversation or a silent prayer.
May my forgiveness be genuine and wholehearted,
A reflection of the love and compassion that you have shown me.

Divine Creator, I ask for your guidance and strength,
As I embark on this transformative journey of forgiveness.
Grant me the patience and perseverance to navigate the complexities of human relationships,
And the wisdom to embrace forgiveness as a path to greater peace and healing.

I express my gratitude for the lessons forgiveness brings,
And for the opportunity to cultivate a heart filled with compassion.

Thank you for the gift of forgiveness,
And for the boundless love and mercy you extend to us all.
In your compassionate name, I pray,
Amen.

Notes - Personal Prayer

A Prayer for Strength

Divine Creator
I come before you now, acknowledging my human limitations,
And seeking the wellspring of strength that flows from your divine essence.

In moments of weakness and adversity, I call upon your power,
To uplift me, to guide me, and to infuse me with unwavering strength.
Grant me the strength to face the challenges that lie before me,
To overcome obstacles and rise above adversity.

When the weight of life feels heavy upon my shoulders,
Strengthen my spirit, that I may persevere with courage and resilience.
In times of doubt and uncertainty, instill within me a steadfast faith,
That I may trust in your divine plan and find solace in your presence.

Help me to believe in my own abilities, to recognize my inherent worth,
And to embrace the strength that resides within my being.

Grant me the strength to stand firm in my convictions,
To uphold my values and live in alignment with my truth.
When faced with difficult choices or societal pressures,
Empower me to make decisions rooted in integrity and wisdom.

Nurture my emotional strength, that I may navigate the depths of my feelings,
Granting me the courage to face my fears and heal my wounds.
Guide me to find inner peace and balance, even in the midst of turmoil,
And strengthen my heart, that I may love fearlessly and authentically.

In times of physical weakness and illness, be my refuge and my healing balm,
Grant me the strength to endure and to restore my body to wholeness.
Infuse my cells with vitality and resilience, that I may thrive in well-being,
And may my physical strength be a vessel for your divine light.

Divine Creator, I surrender to your boundless strength,
Knowing that through you, I am capable of miracles.

Thank you for the strength that flows through my very being,
And for the continuous support and guidance you provide.

With a humble heart, I embrace the strength you bestow upon me,
And I trust in your unwavering presence in my life.
In your mighty name, I pray,
Amen.

Notes - Personal Prayer

A Prayer for Faith

Divine Creator
I pray now asking for the strength and guidance that faith provides.
In moments of uncertainty and doubt, I turn to you,
Asking for the gift of deep and unwavering faith.

Grant me the courage to surrender control,
To trust in your divine plan and timing.
Help me release the need for immediate answers,
And instead find relief in the faith that all is unfolding as it should.
Strengthen my faith when faced with challenges,
When the path ahead seems unclear or filled with obstacles.

In those moments, remind me that you are by my side,
Guiding me, protecting me, and leading me towards growth.
Fill me with a steadfast belief in your goodness and love,
Even when circumstances may suggest otherwise.

Help me to see the miracles and blessings that surround me,
And to find gratitude in even the smallest of moments.
Grant me the faith to embrace the unknown,
To step into the realm of possibility with unwavering trust.
In moments of change and transition, anchor my soul,
And remind me that you are the constant amidst the ever-shifting tides.
Help me to nurture my faith through prayer and reflection,
To seek your presence in the stillness of my being.

Guide me to find strength in your sacred teachings,
And to draw inspiration from the wisdom of those who came before me.
Divine Creator, I offer my gratitude for the gift of faith,
For the peace and comfort it brings to my soul.
Thank you for the unwavering presence of your love,
And for the assurance that I am never alone on this journey.

I surrender my doubts and fears to your divine care,
And I open my heart to the limitless possibilities that faith brings.
With deep reverence and trust, I pray,
Amen.

Notes - Personal Prayer

A Prayer of Understanding

Divine Creator,
I come before you today, asking for your celestial guidance.

Grant me the clarity of mind and the open heart,
To perceive the truths that lie beyond the surface.
Help me to approach the world with curiosity and humility,
To set aside preconceived notions and biases,
So that I may embrace new perspectives and insights.

Guide me to listen attentively to others,
To truly hear their words and understand their experiences.

Grant me the wisdom to discern between knowledge and wisdom,
To recognize that true understanding extends beyond facts and information.

Help me to integrate knowledge with compassion and empathy,
So that I may grasp the deeper meaning and significance of what I learn.

Teach me to see the interconnectedness of all things,
To understand the intricate web of relationships that shape our world.
Help me to recognize the inherent worth and dignity of every being,
And to approach differences with an open heart and a desire for understanding.

Grant me the patience to navigate complex ideas and concepts,
To delve deeper into subjects that challenge my existing beliefs.
May I find the courage to question and explore,
To let go of certainty and embrace the growth that comes with expanding understanding.

Divine Creator, I surrender my ego and my desire for control,
And instead, I ask for the guidance of your divine wisdom.
Grant me the ability to understand myself more fully,
To explore the depths of my own being and unravel the mysteries within.

I express my gratitude for the opportunities to gain understanding,
For the teachers and mentors who share their wisdom,
And for the challenges that encourage my intellectual and spiritual growth.

Thank you for the gift of understanding, and for the continuous unfolding of knowledge.
With a happy heart and trusting in your divine guidance and infinite wisdom I pray,
Amen.

Notes - Personal Prayer

A Prayer for Freedom

Divine Creator
I speak to you with a burning desire,
Seeking the boundless gift of true freedom.
Grant me the strength and courage to break the chains that bind me,
To soar with wings of confidence and embrace the fullness of life.

Free me from the limitations of fear and doubt,
From the shackles of self-imposed limitations.
Help me to release the burdens of the past,
And to step into the vast expanse of the present moment.

Grant me the freedom to be my authentic self,
To express my truth with boldness and authenticity.
Guide me to release the need for external validation,
And to find confidence and fulfillment from within.

Liberate my mind from the constraints of negative thoughts,
And empower me to cultivate a positive and empowering mindset.
Help me to let go of judgment and criticism,
And to embrace self-compassion and acceptance.

Grant me the freedom to forgive and let go of resentments,
To release the hindrances of anger and bitterness.
May forgiveness become a pathway to healing,
And a gateway to experiencing profound inner freedom.

Guide me towards the freedom of choice,
To make decisions aligned with my highest self.
Grant me discernment and wisdom,
So that I may navigate life's crossroads with grace and clarity.

Divine Creator, I express my gratitude for the gift of freedom,
For the opportunities it brings and the liberation it bestows.
Thank you for the freedom to love and be loved,
And for the boundless possibilities that await on the path of liberation.

With a heart filled with longing, I surrender to your divine guidance,
And I ask for your blessings on my quest towards true freedom.
In your sacred name, I pray,
Amen.

Notes - Personal Prayer

A Prayer of Expansion

Divine Creator
I speak now with an open heart and a yearning for growth,
Seeking your counsel to expand the horizons of my mind.

Endow me with the courage to step beyond the boundaries of familiarity,
And embark on a journey of profound intellectual and spiritual exploration.

Open the doors of perception and expand my consciousness,
So that I may embrace new ideas, insights, and perspectives.
Help me to break free from the limitations of my current knowledge,
And to embrace the vastness of the universe and its wonders.

Grant me the ability to question and challenge,
To seek truth with an insatiable curiosity.

Guide me to uncover deeper layers of understanding,
And to integrate knowledge into my being with wisdom and discernment.
Nurture my thirst for knowledge and intellectual growth,
That I may continuously learn and expand my understanding.

Bless me with teachers and mentors who inspire and challenge me,
And surround me with a community of like-minded seekers.

Grant me the humility to recognize that true wisdom lies in recognizing how little I know,
And to approach every new learning opportunity with an open and humble heart.

Help me to embrace the discomfort of growth and transformation,
Knowing that it is through expansion that I discover my true potential.

Divine Creator, I express my gratitude for the gift of a curious mind,
For the capacity to think, question, and explore.
Thank you for the vast universe of knowledge that surrounds us,
And for the opportunities to expand my mind and deepen my understanding.

With a humble heart and an eagerness for growth,
I surrender to your divine guidance and wisdom.
May my mind expand like the vastness of the cosmos,
And may my journey of intellectual exploration be a testament to your divine presence.
In your infinite name, I pray,
Amen.

Notes - Personal Prayer

A Prayer of Purpose

Divine Creator
I speak to you now with an open heart,
Asking for your guidance to discover my true purpose in this life.
Bestow upon me the clarity and insight needed as I continue on this sacred quest,
That I may find meaning and fulfillment in the path I walk.

Help me to recognize the unique gifts and talents you have blessed me with,
And to cultivate them in service to others and the world.

Guide me towards activities and pursuits that ignite my passion,
And align with the values that resonate deep within my soul.

Grant me the wisdom to listen to the whispers of my heart,
To discern the calling that beckons me towards my purpose.

Help me to let go of external expectations and societal pressures,
And to follow the authentic yearnings of my innermost being.
In moments of doubt and uncertainty, provide me with reassurance,
Reminding me that my purpose may unfold in mysterious and unexpected ways.

Grant me the patience and perseverance to navigate the twists and turns,
Trusting that each experience is a stepping stone towards my ultimate purpose.
Help me to embrace the journey of self-discovery,
To explore the depths of my being and uncover my true essence.

Guide me to release limiting beliefs and fears that hold me back,
And to step into the fullness of my potential with courage and confidence.

Divine Creator, I express my gratitude for the gift of purpose,
For the opportunity to contribute my unique light to the world.
Thank you for the lessons, experiences, and relationships that shape my path,
And for the continuous support and guidance you provide.

With a humble heart and an open spirit,
I surrender to your divine plan and purpose for my life.
Grant me the strength and discernment to live in alignment with my true calling,
And to make a meaningful difference in the lives of others.

In your sacred name, I pray,
Amen.

Notes - Personal Prayer

A Prayer of Power

Divine Creator
Please grant me the clarity of mind and the strength of spirit,
To harness and utilize power for the highest level of good for all.
Empower me to embrace my own inner power,
To recognize the strength and potential that flows through my being.

Guide me to use this power responsibly and ethically,
To uplift and inspire others, and to create positive change in the world.
Help me to release any fears or insecurities that diminish my power,
And to step into the fullness of my abilities and potential.

Grant me the courage to overcome obstacles and challenges,
And to persevere in the face of adversity with unwavering determination.
Divine Creator, I surrender my ego and attachments,
And invite your divine power to flow through me.

Infuse me with the power of love and compassion,
So that I may use my influence to uplift and support those in need.

Guide me to align my power with divine wisdom,
To make decisions that honor the interconnectedness of all beings.
Help me to recognize the inherent worth and dignity of every soul,
And to use my power to advocate for justice, equality, and peace.

Grant me the humility to wield power with humility,
To acknowledge the contributions of others and to collaborate harmoniously.
Protect me from the temptations of power for personal gain,
And keep me grounded in the principles of integrity and authenticity.

Divine Creator, I express my gratitude for the opportunity to make a positive impact in the world.
Thank you for entrusting me with this responsibility,
And for the continuous guidance and support you provide.
With a humble heart and a sense of purpose,
I surrender to your divine power and seek to be an instrument of your will.

Guide me to use my power in alignment with divine wisdom,
And to create a world where love, compassion, and harmony prevail.
In your mighty name, I pray,
Amen.

Notes - Personal Prayer

A Prayer for Healing

Divine Creator
I speak to you with a heart burdened by pain and suffering,
Asking for your divine presence and influence to guide me on the path of healing.

Grant me the strength and courage to face my pain,
And the wisdom to navigate the journey of healing.
Pour your healing light upon me, soothing my wounds,
And envelop me in the warmth of your divine love.

Help me to release the grip of past hurts and traumas,
And to embrace the transformative power of healing.
Grant me the courage to confront my pain,
To acknowledge its existence and honor its lessons.
Guide me to find the necessary support and resources,
To heal and integrate my experiences into wisdom and growth.

Nurture my emotional well-being, that I may find inner peace,
And cultivate self-compassion to heal the wounds of self-judgment.
Help me to forgive myself and others,
And to release the confinements of resentment and bitterness.
Grant me the strength to open my heart to forgiveness,
To let go of grudges and embrace the freedom it brings.

Guide me to heal broken relationships, if it is for the highest good,
Or to find solace and closure within myself, if reconciliation is not possible.
Support me in healing my body, mind, and spirit,
From any physical ailments or imbalances that cause pain.

Guide me to the right treatments, therapies, and practices,
That brings holistic healing and restores my well-being.

Divine Creator, I express my gratitude for the gift of healing,
For the capacity of the human spirit to mend and transform.
Thank you for the lessons that pain has taught me,
And for the opportunity to emerge stronger and more resilient.
With an open vessel, I walk through the door of your healing light,
Trusting in the process and allowing your love to guide me.

May the power of your healing energy flow through me,
Restoring wholeness, peace, and joy to every aspect of my being.
This is what I pray,
Amen.

Notes - Personal Prayer

A Prayer for Fun

Divine Creator
I speak to you now to express myself with a desire to infuse my life with more fun and playfulness.
Give me the guidance and inspiration to create moments of pure delight and lightheartedness.
Help me to embrace the childlike spirit within me,
And to cultivate a sense of wonder and joy in every experience.

Help me to have the courage to let go of seriousness and expectations,
And to surrender to the pure joy of the present moment.
Remind me to keep the eternal perspective of life when I become overwhelmed
By everyday worldly stresses.

Guide me to release any worries that weigh me down,
And to welcome laughter and happiness into my life.
Inspire me to explore new adventures and experiences,
To step outside of my comfort zone and discover hidden treasures of fun.

Guide me towards activities that bring me genuine pleasure,
And allow me to express my authentic self without inhibition.
Help me to find humor in life's challenges and imperfections,
And to approach setbacks with a lighthearted and resilient spirit.

Grant me the ability to see the beauty and joy that surrounds me,
Even in the simplest and most ordinary of moments.
Bless me with the company of joyful and uplifting souls,
Who radiate positivity and encourage a spirit of playfulness.

Guide me to create connections and build relationships,
That are filled with shared laughter and cherished memories.

Divine Creator, I express my gratitude for the gift of laughter,
For the ability to experience pure joy and lightness of being.

Thank you for the moments of fun and the smiles that brighten my days,
And for the opportunities to create more fun and laughter in the world.
With a heart filled with anticipation, I surrender to your divine guidance,
And invite more fun and playfulness into my life.

May I embrace the beauty of laughter and find delight in every experience.
For these things I pray,
Amen.

Notes - Personal Prayer

A Prayer for a New Career Path

Divine Creator
I come before you with an open heart,
Seeking your wisdom and blessings as I transition on a new career path.

Grant me the clarity to discern my true passions and talents,
And the courage to pursue a vocation that aligns with my soul's calling.

Guide me to uncover the hidden depths of my skills and abilities,
And to recognize the unique contributions I can make in the world.

Help me to explore new avenues and opportunities,
And to discover a career that brings fulfillment, purpose, and abundance.
Grant me the confidence to step outside of my comfort zone,
And to embrace the challenges and growth that accompany a new journey.

Support me in overcoming obstacles and setbacks,
And in persevering with resilience and determination.
Open doors of opportunity and connect me with the right mentors and allies,
Who can provide guidance and support along my career path.

Help me to build a network of like-minded individuals,
Who inspire and uplift me as I pursue my professional aspirations.
Grant me the wisdom to make sound decisions,
To choose a career that aligns with my values and resonates with my soul.

Guide me to a vocation where I can make a positive impact,
And contribute my unique gifts and talents to the betterment of others and the world.
Divine Creator, I express my gratitude for the opportunity of a fresh start,
For the ability to redefine and shape my professional journey.

Thank you for the lessons and experiences that have led me to this point,
And for the continuous support and guidance you provide.

With a peaceful heart and an open mind I pray,
Amen.

Notes - Personal Prayer

A Prayer to be a Boss

Divine Creator
I speak to you from my heart,
Please grant me the courage to be my own boss,
And the determination to build a successful and fulfilling business.

Guide me to uncover my unique talents and passions,
And to transform them into a thriving enterprise.

Help me to cultivate the mindset of an empowered entrepreneur,
Embracing challenges as opportunities for growth and innovation.
Grant me the clarity to make beneficial decisions,
To set realistic goals and create effective strategies.

Help me to navigate the turbulent waters of business,
And to adapt to the ever-changing landscape with resilience and agility.
Bless me with the resources and support I need,
To bring my business vision to fruition.

Connect me with mentors, advisors, and collaborators,
Who can offer guidance and expertise along my entrepreneurial journey.

Grant me the ability to serve others with integrity and compassion,
To create products and services that uplift and enrich the lives of consumers.

Help me to build a business that aligns with my values,
And contributes to the well-being of my customers, employees, and the community.

Guide me to maintain a healthy work-life balance,
To nurture my well-being and sustain my entrepreneurial spirit.
Help me to find joy and fulfillment in every aspect of my business,
And to create a harmonious environment where passion and purpose thrive.

Divine Creator, I express my gratitude for the opportunity to be my own boss,
For the freedom and responsibility that entrepreneurship brings.
Thank you for the gifts of creativity and resourcefulness,
And for the abundance that flows through the world of business.
With a determined spirit I ask my business be a vehicle for growth, success, and contribution,
And may it bring prosperity and fulfillment to both myself and others.
In your abundant name, I pray,
Amen.

Notes - Personal Prayer

A Prayer of Creativity

Divine Creator
I come to you with an open heart and burning desire to awaken my creative spirit.

Allow me the inspiration to tap into the wellspring of creativity that resides within myself.
Help me to embrace the freedom of self-expression,
And to explore the limitless possibilities of my imagination.

Release me from the constraints of self-doubt and fear,
And ignite the spark of creativity that lives within my soul.

Guide me to break free from the status quo so I can
embrace the unconventional and uniqueness of my spirit.

Gift me the courage to step into the unknown,
To venture beyond the familiar and to take risks in the pursuit of creativity.
Free me from all expectations and judgment,
And ignite the fire of inspiration that moves through me.

Nurture my creative endeavors with patience and perseverance,
And teach me to find joy and fulfillment in the process of creation.
Remind me to cultivate a sense of playfulness and curiosity,
And to approach each creative endeavor with childlike wonder.
Grant me the clarity of vision and the clarity of expression,
That I may communicate my ideas and emotions with authenticity and impact.

Challenge me to embrace my mistakes and failures as stepping stones to growth which they are,
And to learn from them with humility and resilience.
Divine Creator, I express my gratitude for the gift of creativity, and I'm mesmerized by your own perfect
system of creation seen everyday.
Thank you for the countless forms of creative expression that surround me,
And for the opportunities to explore and expand my own creative potential.

May my creativity flow freely and authentically,
And may it bring joy, inspiration, and transformation to myself and others.
In your creative glory, I pray,
Amen.

Notes - Personal Prayer

A Prayer for Happiness

Divine Creator
I speak to you now from my heart to yours.
Asking for your blessing and support to create more happiness in my life.
Please allow me the wisdom to recognize the true sources of joy,
And the courage to cultivate a mindset of gratitude and positivity.

Teach me to embrace the power of the present moment,
To let go of worries about the past and fears about the future.

Help me to find happiness in the simple pleasures of life,
And to appreciate the beauty that surrounds me each day.

Give me the strength to release negative patterns and limiting beliefs,
And to replace them with thoughts of love, kindness, and abundance.

Help me to nurture loving relationships and connections,
And to cultivate a supportive and uplifting social circle.

Help me to prioritize self-care and well-being,
To honor my physical, mental, and emotional needs first for the
Stronger I am, the greater impact I can have on others.
Guide me to engage in activities that bring me joy and fulfillment,
And to make time for hobbies, passions, and moments of relaxation.

Grant me the grace to forgive myself and others,
To let go of grudges and resentments that weigh on my heart.
Help me to cultivate compassion and understanding,
And to approach challenges and conflicts with an open heart.
In your eternal glory, I pray,
Amen.

Notes - Personal Prayer

A Prayer of Health

Divine Creator
I'm coming to you now with an open heart,
seeking your guidance and blessings for a more vibrant, healthy and balanced well-being.
Grant me insight into how I can honor and nurture my physical body, emotional being
and give me the strength to make choices that promote my overall wellness.

Guide me to intuitively listen to the signals of my body,
To understand its needs and respond with love and care.

Help me to cultivate habits that nourish and support my health,
Including wholesome nutrition, regular exercise, and restful sleep.

Support me with the discipline required to release unhealthy patterns,
And to embrace a lifestyle that promotes vitality and balance.

Guide me to let go of harmful substances or behaviors,
And to embrace practices that cultivate holistic well-being.
Bless me with mental and emotional clarity,
And teach me to manage stress and negative emotions effectively.

Help me to cultivate a positive mindset,
And to foster inner peace and resilience in the face of challenges.
Grant me the courage to seek support and guidance when needed,
To reach out to healthcare professionals and experts in the field.

Show me the right resources and treatments,
To heal and restore my body, mind, and spirit.

Divine Creator, I express my thanks for the ability to heal,
For the miracle of life and the vitality that sustains me.
Thank you for the intricate workings of my body,
And for the continuous support and healing energy you provide.

With a gentle heart and a commitment to self-care,
I accept your divine guidance and wisdom.
May my body be a temple of health and life,
And may I be an instrument of well-being and inspiration to others.
In your healing name, I pray,
Amen.

Notes - Personal Prayer

A Prayer for Wealth

Divine Creator
I speak to you now with a sincere heart,
Asking for your direction and blessings to attract and create more wealth in my life.
Please instill in me the clarity to align my thoughts and actions with prosperity,
And the courage to embrace opportunities that lead to financial abundance.

Lead me on a growing path, to recognize and overcome any limiting beliefs or patterns,
That may hinder my ability to attract and receive wealth.
Help me to cultivate a mindset of abundance and gratitude,
And to release any fears or scarcity mentality that holds me back.

Grant me the insight to recognize and seize opportunities,
That align with my values and contribute to my financial growth.
Teach me to make wise decisions and investments,
That bring long-term stability and prosperity into my life.

Bless me with the discipline to manage my resources wisely,
To save, invest, and spend in alignment with my goals.

Show me how to create multiple streams of income,
And to find fulfillment in the pursuit of my financial dreams.

Grant me the courage to step outside of my comfort zone,
To embrace new ventures and take calculated risks.
Help me to learn from failures and setbacks,
And to persevere with resilience and determination.

Divine Creator, I express my gratitude for the abundance that already surrounds me,
For the opportunities and blessings that flow into my life.
Thank you for the resources and talents you have bestowed upon me,
And for the continuous support and guidance you provide.

With a happy heart and a commitment to financial well-being,
I trust in your divine guidance, wisdom and timing.
May I attract wealth with integrity and use it to create positive change,
For myself, my loved ones, and the greater good of all.
In your abundant power, I pray,
Amen.

Notes - Personal Prayer

A Prayer of Improvement

Divine Creator
I ask for your guidance and help to improve my relationships.
Allow me the wisdom to cultivate loving and harmonious connections,
And the courage to heal and grow within my interactions with others.

Help me to increase my understanding of myself,
To become aware of my patterns, triggers, and areas for growth.

Help me to develop more self-compassion and self-love,
So that I may present my best self to my relationships.
Grant me the patience and empathy to truly listen,
To honor the experiences and perspectives of others.

Teach me to communicate with more kindness and authenticity,
And to express myself with clarity and compassion.

Bless me with forgiveness and the ability to let go,
To release past hurts and resentments that hinder my relationships.

Support me to approach conflicts and disagreements with an open heart,
And to seek understanding and resolution with humility and grace.
Grant me the humility to accept my own imperfections,
And to extend grace and acceptance to those around me.

Help me to celebrate the unique gifts and strengths of others,
And to support their growth and well-being.

Divine Creator, I express my thanks for all the beautiful relationships,
For the connections and bonds that enrich my life.

Thank you for the lessons and opportunities to learn and grow,
And for the continuous support and love you provide.
With a humble heart and a commitment to love,
I trust in your divine guidance and wisdom.

May my relationships be filled with love, respect, and understanding,
And may they bring joy, growth, and fulfillment to all involved.
For this I pray,

Amen.

Notes - Personal Prayer

A Prayer of Dedication

Divine Creator
I offer this prayer in dedication and honor to align myself with your divine presence.
Grant me the strength and courage to walk the path of purpose,
And to live a life that reflects your love, wisdom, and grace.

I dedicate my thoughts to the pursuit of truth and enlightenment,
In seeking knowledge that expands my understanding of the world and myself.

Guide my mind towards clarity and discernment,
That I may navigate life's challenges with wisdom and insight.
I dedicate my words to the power of kindness and compassion,
And to speak words that uplift, heal, and inspire others.
Help me to choose my words wisely and to listen attentively,
That my communication may foster connection, understanding, and harmony.

I dedicate my actions to serving my highest self,
To engaging in acts of love, generosity, and selflessness.
Guide me to be a source of support, comfort, and inspiration to others,
And to contribute to the well-being and upliftment of all beings.

I dedicate my heart to the cultivation of gratitude and love,
To nurture a deep connection with the divine and with all living beings.
Grant me the capacity to love unconditionally,
And to radiate compassion, forgiveness, and acceptance in all that I do.

I dedicate my life to the realization of my soul's purpose,
To embrace the unique gifts and talents you have bestowed upon me.
Guide me towards fulfilling my highest potential,
And to make a positive impact in the world with my actions, thoughts, and words.

Divine Creator, I express my deepest gratitude for the blessings and guidance you provide,
For the love and support that surround me on this sacred journey.
Thank you for the opportunities to learn, grow, and serve,
And for the infinite grace that guides me every step of the way.

With an open heart and a soul devoted to your divine will,
I trust myself to your loving presence and guidance.
May this prayer of dedication be a constant reminder,
That I am an instrument of your divine love and light in the world.
In your sacred name, I pray,
Amen.

Notes - Personal Prayer

A Prayer of Peace

Divine Creator
I speak to you with a heart full of love,
Asking for your help to cultivate more internal peace.
Please award me the wisdom to find stillness amidst life's storms,
And the strength to anchor myself in the peace that resides within.

Show me how to release the burdens of worry and fear,
And to trust more of the flow of your divine grace and serenity.
Help me to quiet the noise of my mind,
And to embrace the silence where peace can blossom.

Grant me the clarity to accept what I cannot change,
And the courage to change what I can.
Guide me to let go of attachments and expectations,
And to find peace in embracing the present moment as it is.

Bless me with self-compassion and forgiveness,
To heal the wounds that disrupt my inner peace.
Help me to release judgments and resentments,
And to extend the same compassion to others.

Grant me the freedom to detach from outcomes,
And to trust in the divine plan unfolding in my life.
Guide me to surrender control and find peace in just being,
Knowing that all is well and that I am supported.

Divine Creator, I express my love for the gift of inner peace,
For the many blessings and serenity that nourish my soul.
Thank you for the reminder that peace resides within me,
And for the continuous support and love you provide.

May my inner peace radiate outwards,
Touching the lives of others and creating a ripple of peace in the world.
In your eternal greatness, I pray,
Amen.

Notes - Personal Prayer

A Prayer of Evolution

Divine Creator
I speak now asking for your help to embrace the path of self-evolution.
Please give me the wisdom to recognize my opportunities for growth,
And the courage to step into the unknown with faith and resilience.

Show me my weaknesses and areas that need development,
Teach me how to release old patterns and unhealthy traits,
And to embrace a mindset of expansion and possibility.

Help me to let go of attachments and expectations,
And to trust in the natural flow of growth and change.

Grant me the strength to face my fears and challenges,
And to learn from them with grace and perseverance.
Teach me to embrace discomfort as a catalyst for transformation,
And to welcome the lessons that come with each experience.
Bless me with self-awareness and self-compassion,
To nurture my inner growth with kindness and acceptance.

Help me to cultivate a deeper understanding of myself,
And to align my thoughts, words, and actions with my highest potential.
Grant me the humility to seek guidance and wisdom from others,
To learn from their experiences and perspectives.

Show me how to surround myself with uplifting and supportive influences,
And to engage in practices that inspire and nourish my soul.

Divine Creator, I express my gratitude for the gift of evolution,
For the opportunities to learn, evolve, and become more.
Thank you for the continuous support and guidance you provide,
And for the divine spark of growth that resides within me.

With a happy heart and a commitment to my own evolution,
I believe in your divine timing and wisdom.
May I embrace change and growth with a welcoming invitation and resilience,
And may my evolution bring forth positive transformation in myself and the world.
In your glory I pray,
Amen.

Notes - Personal Prayer

A Prayer of Humility

Divine Creator
I pray to you with a clear mind and open heart,
Asking for your blessings to further develop the virtue of humility.

Allow me the knowledge to recognize the interconnectedness of all beings,
And the strength to embrace a mindset of reverence, openness, and gratitude.
Teach me to release the ego's need for validation and recognition,
And to embrace a posture of humility that honors the inherent worth of all.

Help me to acknowledge and appreciate the contributions of others,
And to value their perspectives, talents, and experiences.
Present me the opportunities to listen to others with an open heart and mind,
To truly hear the wisdom and insights shared by those around me.

Allow me to learn from diverse voices and perspectives,
And to humbly accept that my own understanding is limited and incomplete.

Unlock within me the willingness to admit my mistakes and shortcomings,
And the courage to take responsibility for my actions and their impact.
Help me to learn from failures and setbacks,
And to view them as opportunities for growth and self-reflection.

Grant me the grace to serve others with humility,
To extend kindness, compassion, and support without expecting anything in return.
Show me why it's important to treat each person I encounter with respect and dignity.

Divine Creator, I express my gratitude for the reminder that we are all part of a greater whole.
Thank you for the lessons that humble my spirit and expand my understanding.
With a gracious heart and a commitment to walk the path of humility,
I kneel before your divine guidance and acceptance.

May humility be the foundation of my thoughts, words, and actions,
And may it foster unity, compassion, and love in myself and the world.
In your humble name I pray,
Amen.

Notes - Personal Prayer

A Prayer of Sharing

Divine Creator
I come to you now with a peaceful heart,
Asking for your blessing to cultivate even more of a sharing spirit.
Humble me with your all-knowing wisdom to recognize the abundance in my life,
And the courage to extend a helping hand to those in need.

Push me to be attentive to the needs of others,
To see their struggles, pain, and longing for connection.
Help me to open my heart and share my resources, time, and love,
To bring comfort, support, and joy into the lives of those around me.

Bless me with a spirit of generosity and selflessness,
To give without expecting anything in return.

Show me the importance to share not only material possessions,
But also kindness, compassion, and understanding.

Grant me the humility to ask for help myself,
To recognize that I too am in need of the love and support of others.
Allow me to learn how to create spaces of trust and vulnerability,
Where sharing becomes a reciprocal act of love and connection.

Lead me in making meaningful contributions to the welfare of my community,
To support initiatives that uplift the vulnerable
Where sharing becomes a collective commitment to the greater good.

Divine Creator, I pray with love and gratefulness for all the blessings in my life,
For the resources and opportunities that I have been given.
Thank you for the continuous support and love you provide,
And for the reminder that sharing is a sacred act of compassion.

May my actions be a reflection of your unconditional love,
And may the spirit of sharing spread kindness, compassion, and joy to all.
In your loving name, I pray,
Amen.

Notes - Personal Prayer

A Prayer of Mercy

Divine Creator
I ask you now for your support and help.
Please allow me the strength to extend grace and forgiveness,
And to cultivate a heart of compassion and understanding.
Guide me to recognize the inherent worth and dignity of all beings,
To see beyond their faults and shortcomings.

Help me to release my judgments and prejudices,
And to approach others with empathy and kindness.

Bless me with the ability to forgive those who have wronged me,
To let go of resentment and seek reconciliation.
Guide me to heal the wounds that hinder my capacity for mercy,
And to extend forgiveness not only to others but also to myself.

Allow me to access my higher self to detach from the pain and suffering inflicted by others,
To be a source of comfort, support, and peace.
Help me to be present with those who are hurting,
And to offer compassion and understanding without judgment.

Divine Creator, I express my thanks creating the quality of mercy,
For the unconditional love and compassion you show towards me.
Thank you for the continuous support and guidance you provide,
And for the reminder that mercy is a transformative force in the world.

With an open heart and a commitment to becoming more merciful,
I put my trust and remain open to your divine guidance.

May my actions reflect your love and boundless mercy,
And may the spirit of mercy ripple through me, touching all beings.
In your name I pray,
Amen.

Notes - Personal Prayer

A Prayer for Family

Divine Creator
I pray to you now with a happy heart and clear mind,
Asking for your help and direction in the matters of family,
as I'd like to prioritize and cherish them even more.

Help me prioritize my life and to recognize the preciousness of these relationships,
And the commitment to spend quality time with my loved ones.
Guide me to create a harmonious and nurturing environment at home,
Where love, laughter, and understanding flourish.

Help me to be present and attentive to the needs of my family,
To listen deeply and offer my support and encouragement.
Bless me with the ability to set aside distractions and obligations,
To make space in my schedule for meaningful moments with my family.

Show me how to prioritize their well-being and happiness,
And to create lasting memories that strengthen our bond.
Help me develop the patience even more to embrace the imperfections and challenges,
To navigate disagreements with love and respect for everyone included.

Help me to foster a sense of unity and belonging within my family,
Where each member feels valued, understood, and cherished.
Guide me to be mindful of the passage of time,
To recognize the fleeting nature of moments spent together.

Help me to seize the opportunities to connect and engage,
And to treasure the joy and love we share as a family.

Divine Creator, I express my eternal gratefulness for the gift of my family,
For the love and support that surrounds me.
Thank you for the continuous blessings and examples in my life you provide,
And for the reminder to prioritize and invest in these sacred relationships.

With a commitment to improving the bonds within my family,
I trust in your judgment and all-knowing wisdom.

May I create a sanctuary of love and unity within my home,
And may the time spent with my family be filled with joy, growth, and deep connection.
In your loving name I pray,
Amen.

Notes - Personal Prayer

A Prayer of Leadership

Divine Creator
I humbly speak to you, seeking your expertise,
As I urge you to learn how to be a wise leader.
Please sharpen my power of discernment between right and wrong,
To make decisions that uphold truth, justice, and integrity.
Guide me to lead with clarity and vision,
To see the bigger picture and inspire others to share in the vision.

Help me to navigate complexities of any challenge with calmness and intelligence,
And to make choices that benefit not only the present but also the future.

Bless me with the ability to listen deeply and empathetically,
To understand the perspectives and needs of those I lead.
Guide me to create an inclusive and supportive environment,
Where every voice is heard and valued, and collaboration thrives.

Allow me the strength of humility to admit my own limitations and seek guidance,
To surround myself with wise advisors and mentors.
Help me to learn from the experiences and teachings of others,
And to continuously grow in knowledge and understanding.

Bless me with the courage to take risks and learn from failures,
To view setbacks as opportunities for growth and improvement.
Guide me to lead by example, demonstrating resilience and perseverance,
And inspiring others to overcome challenges with flexibility and determination.

Divine Creator, I express my desire for the opportunity to lead,
For the trust placed in me to guide and inspire others.,
Your example is a constant reminder to lead with love, compassion, and humility.
May I lead with integrity, empathy, and discernment,
And may my leadership inspire positive change and growth in myself and others.
In your wise name, I pray,
Amen.

Notes - Personal Prayer

A Prayer of Adventure

Divine Creator
I speak to you now in a spirit of curiosity and wonder,
I desire to explore new locations, new cultures and new people.

Help me muster the courage to step outside my comfort zone,
And the openness to embrace the transformative power of new experiences.
Guide me to new lands and cultures, To encounter diverse perspectives
and expand my understanding of the world.

Allow me to immerse myself in the beauty and richness of unfamiliar places,
And to appreciate the interconnectedness of all humanity.
Bless me with open eyes and an open heart,
To witness the wonders of nature and the creations of humanity.

Teach me to appreciate the magnificence of landscapes and cityscapes,
And to honor the sacredness of each place I encounter.
Grant me the humility to learn from the people I meet,
To listen to their stories and embrace the knowledge they share.

Help me to connect with fellow travelers and locals alike,
And to foster connections that transcend language and cultural barriers.
Guide me to travel responsibly and sustainably,
To respect the environment, cultures, and traditions of the places I visit.
Help me to leave a positive impact wherever I go,
And to contribute to the preservation of our planet and its diverse heritage.

Divine Creator, I express my thankfulness for the gift of exploration and for this amazing home planet called
Earth. I appreciate any and all opportunities to broaden my horizons and enrich my soul..

May my travels be filled with awe, inspiration, and growth,
And may the experiences I encounter shape me into a more compassionate,enlightened and evolved being.
For my gratitude and desire to experience your creations I pray,

Amen.

Notes - Personal Prayer

A Prayer of Excellence

Divine Creator
I pray now with reverence and humility,
Asking for your direction and support in the spirit of excellence.
I need help to further develop the unique gifts and talents within me,
And the strength to explore and flush them out to their fullest potential.

Guide me to strive for excellence in all that I do,
To set high standards and pursue them with passion and dedication.
Help me to embrace a growth mindset,
Continuously seeking opportunities for learning, improvement, and mastery.

Bless me with the ability to overcome challenges and obstacles,
To persevere in the face of any adversity.
Guide me to learn from failure, to learn the lesson once,
And to view them as stepping stones on the path to excellence.

Teach me the discipline to maintain focus and commitment,
To prioritize my time and energy towards meaningful pursuits.
Help me to honor my responsibilities and obligations,
And to approach each task with a spirit of excellence and integrity.

Bless me with the humility to recognize the contributions of others,
To appreciate their talents and achievements without comparison or envy.
Guide me to collaborate and learn from those who excel in different areas,
And to celebrate the collective pursuit of excellence within my various teams.

Divine Creator, I express my desire for the opportunity to further develop my greatness,
Your example is a reminder that excellence is not a destination, but a lifelong journey.
With a humble heart and a commitment to excellence,
I strive to lead a balanced and excellent life that is full of love and accomplishment.

May my thoughts, words, and actions reflect the pursuit of excellence,
And may the impact I make in the world be a testament to your boundless grace.
For these things, I pray,
Amen.

Notes - Personal Prayer

A Prayer of Courage

Divine Creator
I pray to you now with a calm mind and open heart,
Asking you to help me with matters of courage.

Please give me the courage to face my fears and step into the unknown,
Give me the strength to persevere in the face of uncertainty and to have faith
That what is meant to be will be.

Guide me to recognize that true courage lies within,
And that I am capable of overcoming any obstacle that comes my way.
Help me to trust in my abilities and innate resilience,
And to believe in the potential that lies dormant within me.

Bless me with the courage to pursue my dreams and aspirations,
To take bold and decisive actions towards my goals.
Teach me to listen to my intuition and to trust my gut.
Allow me the opportunity to have the courage to follow my own path, even if it diverges from the norm.
Give me the courage to stand up for what is right,
To speak out against injustice and defend the vulnerable.
Help me to embody compassion and empathy in my interactions,
And to use my voice to advocate for positive change.

Bless me with the courage to forgive and let go of control,
To release grudges and embrace the healing power of compassion.

Divine Creator, I express my thanks for the gift of courage,
For the strength and fortitude you instill within me.

Support me so I can face any challenge with unwavering courage.
With a humble heart and a commitment to courage,
I trust in your divine guidance and example.
May I walk the path of courage with bravery,
And may my actions inspire courage in others.
For this I pray,
Amen.

Notes - Personal Prayer

A Prayer of Travel

Divine Creator
I pray now with a thirst for travel, I wish to experience the wonders of this world.
Allow me the opportunities to explore diverse lands and unfamiliar cultures,
To encounter the beauty and diversity that exists beyond my own horizons.

Help me embrace the richness and interconnectedness of your earthly creation,
And to appreciate the wisdom and lessons each place has to offer.

Bless me with open eyes and an open heart,
To behold the awe-inspiring beauty and breathtaking diversity of your wonders.

Guide me to walk ancient paths, to explore hidden gems,
And to immerse myself in the vibrant colors of different human experiences.
Release me from my preconceived notions and expand my humility
So I may learn from the people I meet,
To listen to their stories and honor their traditions.
.
Guide me to travel to where I am meant to experience,
To tread lightly upon the Earth and respect the environments I encounter.
Help me to be mindful of the communities I visit,
And to contribute to their well-being and preservation.

Divine Creator, I express my gratitude for life and vehicle for growth travel provides,
For the opportunities to expand my horizons and deepen my understanding
Of myself and others.

May my journeys be filled with wonder, growth, and connection,
And may the experiences I encounter enrich my soul and broaden my perspective.
In adventurous spirit I pray,
Amen.

Notes - Personal Prayer

A Prayer of Learning

Divine Creator
I pray now to your infinite wisdom and humbly ask for your assistance in developing my own.
I ask to remain on my path of continuous learning.
To further ignite my curiosity to explore the depths of knowledge,
And the humility to acknowledge that there is always more to discover.

Teach me to embrace each day as a new opportunity,
To expand my understanding, skills, and perspectives.
Support me to live a life inspired with an endless thirst for knowledge and experience.
Help me approach each learning experience with a free mind and a willing spirit.

Develop me into a person with the ability to learn from every and any person I encounter,
To listen attentively and gain insight from their unique stories.
Allow me to see the valuable lessons hidden in every moment.

Bless me with discipline and focus,
To invest my time and energy in meaningful pursuits while reminding me
to prioritize learning amidst the demands of daily life.
Help me create a sacred space for intellectual and personal growth.

Divine Creator, I express my love for learning,
For the ability to expand my current knowledge base and to deepen my understanding.
May I always be open to learning, in every season of life,
And may the knowledge I acquire inspire positive change and serve the greater good.
In your name of eternal wisdom, I pray,
Amen.

Notes - Personal Prayer

A Prayer of Attraction

Divine Creator
I pray to you with an open heart seeking your advice and support towards
manifesting my soul's desires.

Gift me the clarity of intention and unwavering belief,
To align my thoughts and actions with the manifestation of my desires.

Help me understand that I am a co-creator of my reality,
And that I possess the power to shape my own destiny.
Help me to release any doubts or limiting beliefs,
And to embrace the limitless possibilities that lie before me.

Bless me with unwavering faith and trust in your divine timing,
Knowing that what is meant for me will come at the perfect moment.

Teach me to let go of attachment and to trust in the flow of life,
Understanding that the universe will provide all that I need.

Gift me with the foresight to process my true desires,
To align them with the highest level of my soul.
Help me to generate positive thoughts and emotions,
And to radiate the energy of love, gratitude, and abundance.
Allow me entrance into the frequency of manifesting so I can live in a state of creation.

Support me with the courage to take inspired action,
To follow my intuition and pursue my dreams wholeheartedly.
Guide me to make choices aligned with my desires,
And to be open to unexpected opportunities and synchronicities.

Divine Creator, I express my desire to strengthen my power of manifestation,
For the ability to attract and create my desired reality.

Thank you for the continuous blessings your grace provides in my life,
And for the daily reminder that I am a powerful magnet for all that I seek.
With a heart full of passion and a commitment to alignment,
I trust in your timing and celestial powers.
May my intentions and desires manifest in accordance with the highest good,
And may my life be filled with abundance, joy, and fulfillment.
In your greatness I pray,
Amen.

Notes - Personal Prayer

A Prayer of Balance

Divine Creator
I pray now for your help towards living a more balanced life.
Provide me with the clarity needed to navigate the murky waters of life
with insight to harmonize the various aspects of my being.

Help me to embrace the delicate dance of balance,
To honor the needs of my body, mind, and spirit in equal measure.
Help me to prioritize self-care and nourishment,
And to create a sacred space for rest, reflection, and rejuvenation.

Teach me how to better manage my time and energy wisely,
To set boundaries and make choices that support my overall well-being.
Guide me to find harmony between work and leisure,
And to engage in activities that bring joy, fulfillment, and growth.
Grant me the courage to say no when necessary,
To release the pressures of overcommitment and fear of missing out.

Help me gravitate towards having a centered and calm state of being,
Even amidst the busyness and demands of daily life.

Heighten my awareness of my interconnectedness with nature,
To honor the rhythms and cycles that exist in the world and around me.
Protect my being from negative influence and teach me how to remain unaffected by others state of being.
Guide me to seek harmony in my relationships,
While drawing clear boundaries that protect my balance.

Divine Creator, I say thank you for helping me achieve a life of balance,
For the opportunity to find equilibrium in all aspects of my life.
May I embody balance in my thoughts, actions, and choices,
And may my life be an example of divine equilibrium.
In your name of balance, I pray,
Amen.

Notes - Personal Prayer

A Prayer of Ridding Vices

Divine Creator
I come before you with an open heart seeking guidance
In an effort to improve my life as I strive to break free from the chains of addiction.

Please provide me with the strength of commitment and courage to face my struggles, to take accountability
as I embark on the path of recovery.

Guide me to recognize the power of my own choices,
And the capacity within me to overcome this addiction.
Help me to confront the underlying causes and emotions,
And to find healthier ways to cope and find peace.

Bless me with the support and understanding of loved ones,
And surround me with compassionate souls who uplift and inspire.
Guide me to seek professional help and guidance if needed,
To find the resources and tools necessary for my healing journey.

Grant me the perseverance to face the challenges that arise,
And the resilience to bounce back from setbacks along the way.
Help me to embrace the process of healing and transformation,
And to trust in my ability to create a life free from addiction.

Bless me with self-compassion and forgiveness,
To release any guilt or shame that may burden my spirit.
Guide me to generate self-love and acceptance,
And to embrace the inherent worth and dignity within me.

Divine Creator, direct me on my path towards healing and
for the opportunity to reclaim my life and rediscover my true essence.

Thank you for believing in me and allowing me the opportunity to make another choice,
Thank you for the reminder that I am not alone in this journey towards freedom.
With a honest heart and a commitment to transformation,
I trust in your divine guidance and strive to connect to the higher powers.
May I find the strength and resilience to overcome addiction.
In your greatness I pray,
Amen.

Notes - Personal Prayer

A Prayer of Romance

Divine Creator
I pray to you now in the matters of love and connection,
I have a longing in my heart seeking your assistance
and guidance to attract a loving romantic partner.

Provide me with the clarity to understand my true desires,
And the patience to trust in your divine timing.
Teach me to release any fears or hindrances blocking my signal,
And to open myself up to the abundance of love that surrounds me.

Help me to radiate love and positivity from within,
And to become a magnet for a compatible and fulfilling relationship.
Bless me with the insight to discern what truly matters,
To seek a partner who aligns with my values, dreams, and aspirations.

Guide me to create more self-love and self-acceptance,
Knowing that a healthy and nourishing relationship starts within.
Give me the courage to be vulnerable and authentic,
To communicate my needs and desires with clarity and compassion.

Help me to create space in my life for a loving partnership,
And to make room for the beautiful connection that awaits me.
Bless me with the ability to recognize the signs and synchronicities,
That guide me towards the right person for me.

Guide me to be patient and trusting as I navigate this journey,
Knowing that you have a perfect plan in store for my love life.

Thank you for your example of true love and for the daily reminder
that love is a divine force that unites us all.
With a loving heart and a commitment to find love,
May I attract a romantic partner who mirrors my soul,
And may our love be a beacon of success, growth, and mutual support.
In the name of love I pray,
Amen.

Notes - Personal Prayer

A Prayer of Acceptance

Divine Creator
I come before you with an open heart,
Seeking your guidance and support to better accept others.
Provide me with the openness to see beyond differences and judgments,
And to embrace the inherent worth and uniqueness of every soul.
Help me release any need to change or control others,
And to instead approach them with kindness and understanding.
Help me develop more empathy and patience,
And to recognize the struggles and journeys that have shaped each person.

Bless me with the ability to listen deeply and without judgment,
To honor the perspectives and experiences of others.
Help me foster connections built on respect and kindness,
And to create spaces where acceptance flourishes.

Help me to embrace diversity as a source of richness and growth,
And to celebrate the beauty in our shared humanity.
Bless me with the accountability to recognize my own limitations,
And to approach others with a spirit of learning and growth.

Teach me to extend forgiveness and grace to others,
And to foster reconciliation and understanding in moments of conflict.
Divine Creator, I seek to build more community full of
Beautiful souls that enrich my life and the others around them.

May I embrace others with love in all the uniqueness that they are,
And may acceptance become a cornerstone of my relationships and interactions.
For this I pray,
Amen.

Notes - Personal Prayer

A Prayer of Creation

Divine Creator
I pray to you seeking your guidance and support in my desire to create a loving family.
Show me how to create a more nurturing and supportive environment,
Where love, respect, and harmony flourish.
Counsel me to find a partner who shares my dreams and values,
Someone with whom I can build a strong and enduring bond with.

Help me to propagate a relationship built on trust and communication,
Where we can support and uplift each other on this journey of family.
Bless us with the miracle of conceiving and bringing forth life,
Granting us the gift of parenthood and the blessings of children.

Help us to create a loving home where they can thrive in
A protected space which will nurture their growth, happiness, and well-being.
Teach us the strength to overcome challenges and obstacles,
And to face the responsibilities of family with grace, resilience and understanding.

Help us to always prioritize love and connection amidst the busyness of life,
Creating beautiful moments of joy, laughter, and deep bonding.
Bless us with your wisdom to instill values of kindness and compassion,
Teaching our children the importance of empathy and understanding.

Allow our Love to be a beacon of hope and example of yours that
will create a legacy of happiness and success that extends beyond our family.

Divine Creator, I express my desire for the blessing of family and
Ask for the opportunity to prove my worthiness for such a sacred gift.

May we create a family rooted in love and understanding,
And may our journey together be filled with love, happiness, and togetherness.
In your name of love, I pray,
Amen.

Notes - Personal Prayer

A Prayer of Service

Divine Creator
I pray to you now with a desire to further help my fellow man,
I wish to be of more service to others in any way I can.

Provide me with the clarity and awareness to recognize the needs of those around me,
And the decisiveness to act with kindness, empathy, selflessness and action.
Help me see beyond myself and extend a helping hand,
To offer support, love, and compassion to anyone in need.
Help me to listen deeply and without judgment,
And to offer support and understanding to those who are hurting.

Bless me with the ability to see the humanity in every person,
To honor their dignity and worth, regardless of their circumstances.
Guide me to serve without seeking recognition or reward,
And to find fulfillment in the act of giving itself.
Grant me the strength to step outside my comfort zone,
To embrace opportunities for service and acts of kindness.
Help me to use my skills, talents, and resources,
To make a positive impact in the lives of others.

Guide me to collaborate with others in service,
And to foster a spirit of unity and cooperation.
May I be an instrument of love and light,
And may my actions bring comfort, healing, and transformation to those I serve.
In your name of service, I pray,
Amen.

Notes - Personal Prayer

A Prayer of Fulfillment

Divine Creator
I speak to you now with an open heart, open mind and empty vessel
Seeking your advice and support in my pursuit towards pure fulfillment.
Provide me with the introspection to understand my deepest desires,
And the courage to pursue a life that aligns with my soul's calling.

Help me uncover my passions and talents,
And to embrace the unique gifts that reside within me.
Help me discover a sense of purpose and meaning,
And to live each day with intention and authenticity.

Bless me with the insight to discern what truly brings me happiness,
And the willingness to let go of what no longer serves me.
Direct me to seek experiences that nourish my spirit,
And to prioritize activities that ignite a sense of purpose and fulfillment.

Help me to release the need for external validation,
And to find fulfillment in the journey of self-discovery and personal growth.
Provide me with the ability to generate more gratitude and contentment,
To recognize the blessings that already abound in my life.
Teach me to appreciate the present moment,
And to find happiness and fulfillment in the simple pleasures that surround me.

Divine Creator, I want to express my love for this gift of life,
And for the opportunity to seek and find true fulfillment.
I embrace the journey of life and both the challenges and blessings sprinkled along the path.
I now express my desire to level up and ask for you to share the clues that will lead
Me closer to a life of fulfillment.
May I embrace my passions, live with purpose,
And find deep fulfillment in every aspect of my existence.
In your name, I pray,
Amen.

Notes - Personal Prayer

A Prayer of Manifestation

Divine Creator
I come before you with a heart full of hope,
Seeking your divine leadership and assistance in manifesting my desires.
Provide me with the clarity to identify my truest and highest aspirations, big, small, spiritual or worldly,
Give me the confidence to believe in my ability to bring them into reality.

Help me to align my thoughts, beliefs, and actions,
With the energy of abundance, success, and manifestation.
Help me to release any doubts and fears,
And to shift into a mindset of unwavering faith and positivity.

Bless me with the patience to trust in your divine timing,
And the resilience to persevere even in the face of failure.
Guide me to take inspired action towards my goals,
And to remain open to unexpected opportunities that come my way.

Provide me with an acute mind to set clear intentions and visualize my desires,
To create a powerful energetic connection with what I wish to manifest.
Help me to detach from outcomes and trust in your divine plan,
Knowing that you have the ultimate wisdom and understanding.

Bless me with the abundance of resources and support I need,
To bring my desires into fruition for the highest good of all.
Show me how to be in alignment with my soul's purpose,
So that my manifestations serve not only myself but also the greater good.

Divine Creator, I express only gratitude for the power of manifestation you created,
For the ability to co-create my reality with your divine energy.
Thank you for the continuous blessings and guidance you provide,
And for the reminder that I am a powerful vessel of manifestation.

With this pray, may my desires manifest in perfect harmony with your divine plan,
And may my life be a testament to the infinite possibilities that lie within me.
In your glory, I pray,
Amen.

Notes - Personal Prayer

A Prayer for Self-Care

Divine Creator
I pray to you with a grateful and open heart,
Asking for your help and direction to better prioritize my self-care.
Please gift me the confidence to realize my worth and value,
And the strength to honor my needs and well-being.

Teach me how to create a loving relationship with myself,
To treat my body, mind, and spirit with gentleness and support.
Help me to nourish myself with wholesome food and restful sleep,
And to engage in activities that replenish and rejuvenate my soul.
Bless me with the awareness to listen to my body's wisdom,
To heed its signals and honor its boundaries.

Remind me to prioritize self-reflection and inner growth,
Creating space for stillness and self-discovery.
Allow me the courage to set healthy boundaries,
To say no when necessary and to prioritize my own well-being.
Help me to release self-judgment and embrace self-acceptance,
Knowing that I am worthy of love and care just as I am.

Bless me with the ability to forgive myself for past mistakes,
And to release any guilt or shame that weighs me down my spirit.
Show me how to practice self-love and self-forgiveness,
Allowing myself to heal and grow from within.

Divine Creator, I express my deepest gratitude for the gift of life and
for the opportunity to learn how to better care for myself and nurture my soul.
May I honor my needs, nurture my well-being,
And live a life that is balanced, fulfilling, and aligned with my highest level.
In your name, I pray,
Amen.

Notes - Personal Prayer

A Prayer of Intuition

Divine Creator
I come to you now as a soul seeking the further development of my intuition.
Grant me the clarity and spiritual fortitude to recognize the whispers of my inner voice,
And the courage to follow its guidance with unwavering trust.

Help me quiet the noise and distractions of the world around me,
To still my mind and open my heart to the whispers of my soul.
Help me to discern the subtle nudges and intuitive messages sent from above,
And to honor the wisdom that flows from deep within.

Remind me with the strength to trust my instincts,
Even when they seem contrary to logic or societal expectations.
Guide me to release doubt, fear, and uncertainty,
And to step boldly into the path that aligns with my soul's purpose.

Help me to cultivate a deep connection with my intuition,
And to trust it as a guiding compass in every decision I make.
Provide me with the ability to discern the difference between fear and intuition,
To recognize when my intuition is guiding me towards growth and expansion.
Assist me to remain in the divine flow of life not always seen but always felt,
Trusting that my intuition will lead me to the experiences and opportunities I need.

Divine Creator, I express my gratitude for the celestial gift of intuition,
For the inner guidance that leads me towards my highest self and
For implanting this spark and connection that is my tether to you, the creator.

May I continue to listen to the whispers of my intuition, may its signal
And the voice to my ears become louder as I trust in the divine unfolding of my journey.
In your name, I pray,
Amen.

Notes - Personal Prayer

A Prayer of Confidence

Divine Creator
I speak to you now with an open heart, ready to receive, seeking your help and your guidance
To better solidify unwavering self-assurance.
Help me to recognize my inherent worth and embrace my unique qualities.
Show me how to release self-doubt and damaging beliefs,
And how to replace them with a deep sense of self-belief and empowerment.

Bless me with the strength to embrace my greatness and to improve my weaknesses,
To see them as opportunities for growth and for learning.
Remind me to celebrate my accomplishments,
Both big and small, and to recognize my contributions to the world.
Help me let go of comparison and feelings of lack,
As I want to trust in my own abilities and inner wisdom.

Bless me with the foresight to see the beauty and potential within myself,
And to radiate confidence from the depths of my being.
Guide me to speak my truth with conviction and grace,
And to assert myself with kindness and respect.

Grant me the strength to overcome any challenges and setbacks,
To see them as the blessings that they are on my journey towards confidence.

Remind me to embrace the power of positive self-talk and affirmations,
Nurturing a mindset that fosters self-assurance and self-love.

Divine Creator, I ask for your help with further expanding my confidence,
For the ability to stand tall and embrace my authentic self.

May I develop unwavering confidence that shines from within,
And may it empower me to fulfill my highest potential.
In your name, I pray,
Amen.

Notes - Personal Prayer

A Prayer of Generosity

Divine Creator
I speak to you now with a happy heart and a desire to spread more generosity.

I ask for your assistance and guidance to better embrace the spirit of giving.
Help me embody the qualities of selflessness, kindness, and empathy.
I seek to improve as a child of yours, that leads a life of love.

Remind me to recognize the blessings and abundance in my life,
And the importance of sharing them generously with others who are in need.
Bless me with a spirit of open-heartedness and a willingness to give,
Without expecting anything in return.

Allow me an expansive mind to see beyond material possessions,
And to understand that true generosity extends beyond material wealth.
Help me to offer my time, attention, and support to those who require it,
And to create a positive impact in their lives.

Bless me with the awareness to see the interconnectedness of all beings,
And to recognize that when I give, I contribute to the well-being of the world.

Help me shift my beliefs and gear them towards being
generous in my thoughts, words, and actions,
Creating ripples of kindness and love in every interaction.
Help me extend my generosity to those I may not know or understand.

Urge me to foster an inclusive and compassionate mindset,
And to uplift and empower those who are in need.
Boost my connection to the creator and strengthen my signal of love
So I can radiate giving energy in your honor. Protect me from those
That might want to take advantage of this quality and gift me with the
Power of discernment.
Bless me with gratitude for the opportunities to give,
And for the joy that comes from making a positive difference.

Allow me to be a channel of your divine love and abundance,
Touching the lives of others and inspiring generosity in their hearts.

Divine Creator, I express my gratitude for the gift of generosity and
The examples you show me daily.
May I be an instrument of generosity and compassion,
And may my actions inspire others to embrace the spirit of giving.
In your name of love, I pray,
Amen.

Notes - Personal Prayer

A Prayer of Empathy

Divine Creator
I speak to you now as a student and child of yours asking for help to further develop
The quality of empathy.

Help me to embody the qualities of compassion, kindness, and connection
And grant me the opportunities to display such qualities.
Show me how to open my heart to the experiences of others,
To truly listen as I seek to better understand others; their joys and struggles.

Open my mind and heart with the ability to put myself in their shoes,
And to empathize with their emotions and experiences.
Allow me to grow into a human that recognizes the inherent worth of every individual,
And to embrace their humanity with love and acceptance.

Help me to set aside judgment, prejudice, and bias,
And to see the common threads that unite us all.
Bless me with a sensitive and attentive spirit,
To perceive the unspoken words and hidden pains of those around me.
Expand my emotional acuteness so I can read the temperature of others
And my surroundings without speaking a word.

Ignite my celestial signal as a beacon of love that support others
with genuine care and support as I Offer a comforting presence
and a compassionate ear.

Help me to use my voice to amplify the voices of the less fortunate,
And to create a world where empathy and understanding prevail.
Bless me with the ability to forgive and show grace,
To extend empathy even in moments of disagreement or conflict.

Support me in choosing words and actions that uplift and heal,
Building bridges of understanding and fostering reconciliation.

Divine Creator, I express love and desire to develop the gift of empathy,
For the ability to connect deeply with the experiences of others and
To be a force of light and peace in the world.

May I embody empathy in every thought, word, and action,
And may my empathy ripple out, touching lives and igniting change.
In your name of love, I pray,
Amen.

Notes - Personal Prayer

A Prayer of Honesty

Divine Creator
I come before you now as a child of the universe with a desire to become even more honest.
I wish to live a pure existence, free from fabricating or embellishing stories and to be aligned
With the facts of reality.

Support me with your guidance and blessings to live a life of authenticity and truth.
Help me to embrace the qualities of honesty, transparency, and integrity.
Assist me to honor the truth in every aspect of my life,
To speak words that reflect my genuine thoughts and feelings.
Bless me with the courage to be honest with myself and others,
Even in moments when it may be difficult or uncomfortable.

Help me develop the insight to discern between truth and falsehood,
To seek the truth with an open mind and heart.
Help me to let go of deceit, manipulation, and half-truths,
And to embrace the power of honesty as a transformative force.

Support my desire with strength to take responsibility for my actions,
To admit my mistakes and learn from them with humility.
Guide me to live with integrity and honor my commitments,
Being true to my word and following through on my promises.

Train me with compassion to deliver the truth with kindness,
To communicate honestly without causing unnecessary harm.
Help me to foster and radiate a safe and trusting aura,
Where truth can be shared and received with welcomeness and understanding.

Build me with the power to challenge falsehood and injustice,
To stand up for truth and promote transparency in all realms of life.
Guide me to be a beacon of honesty in a world that may be filled with deceit,
And to inspire others to embrace the transformative power of truth.

Divine Creator, I express only a desire to further develop my honest self,
And say thank you for the example you set through others that I may learn from.
Thank you for the many continuous blessings and guidance you provide,
And for the reminder that through honesty, we build trust and harmony.
With a humble heart and a commitment to truth,
I trust in your wisdom.
May I be a vessel of honesty in all that I do,
And may my words and actions reflect the highest truth.
In your name, I pray,
Amen.

Notes - Personal Prayer

A Prayer of Wisdom

Divine Creator,
I speak to you now with a burning desire to acquire more wisdom and become an
Even stronger beacon of light.
Assist me with your guidance and blessings to pull from the deep wisdom within.
Help me to embody the qualities of discernment, insight, and clarity.
Support me in my pursuit to gather more knowledge and understanding,
To learn from the lessons of the past and the teachings of the present.

Bless me with a sponge of a mind and a thirst for wisdom,
That can apply knowledge with discernment.

Grant me a higher ability of understanding to see beyond appearances,
To perceive the deeper truths and underlying meanings in life.
Help me navigate the complexities and deceits of the world with clarity,
Making choices that align with the highest good for all.

Bless me with the ability to listen to my inner voice and gut feelings,
To connect with my intuition and trust its instincts.

Remind me to find stillness and silence amidst the noise,
So I can receive the signals flowing from the depths of my being.

Grant me the patience and peace to recognize that wisdom is a lifelong journey,
And that I am forever a student, always growing and evolving.

Support me to learn from my mistakes and embrace the lessons they offer,
And to share the wisdom gained with compassion and accountability.

Bless me with the confidence to live in alignment with my inner wisdom,
To make choices that honor my values and reflect my highest self.
Guide me to use this wisdom as a tool for healing, justice, and peace,
And to inspire others to awaken their own wisdom that resides within them.

Divine Creator, I am humbled by your creations on earth and perfect system life is,
I only ask for the opportunity to learn more and become more like you.
For the ability to seek truth and navigate life with discernment.
Thank you for the reminder that through wisdom, we find clarity and purpose.

With an empty vessel ready to receive and a commitment to wisdom,
I let go of my timeline and preconceived notions as I trust in your divine guidance and wisdom.

May I embody your wisdom in every thought, word, and action,
And may my wisdom contribute to the well-being of all.
In your name, I pray,
Amen.

Notes - Personal Prayer

A Prayer of Patience

Divine Creator
I pray now as a child of yours seeking help with my further development of patience.
Teach me with your guidance to embody this virtue.
Help me embrace the qualities of serenity, tolerance, and understanding.
When frustrating times tempt me to emotionally react, help me find inner peace.
When amidst the challenges and uncertainties of life give me the strength the remain
An unshakeable force of leadership and peace.

Help me trust in the divine timing of all things.
Provide me with the strength to persevere in times of waiting and adversity,
And to maintain a sense of peace and equanimity in the face of impatience.

Equip me with the insight and internal peace to accept that some things take time,
And that the journey itself holds valuable lessons and growth.
Help me to release the need for instant gratification,
And to find joy and contentment in the process of unfolding.

Improve my ability and capacity to extend patience to others,
To offer understanding and support in their moments of struggle free
From my personal feelings.
Teach me to listen with patience, to withhold judgment,
And to create space for growth and transformation in their lives.

Help me give up personal control and trust in the greater plan,
To let go of the need for immediate results and outcomes.

Clear space in my heart of the distractions that don't serve me
to allow more room for your divine guidance.,

Remind me to appreciate the present moment,
And for the lessons that patience teaches me in each moment.
Remind me to be mindful and fully present,
Embracing the beauty and opportunities that arise in the here and now.

Divine Creator, I come to you as a student asking for help with patience,
For the ability to grow in serenity and endurance.
Thank you for the lessons of patience for its one way we find more inner peace.

May I use your knowledge and my action to embody more patience
in every thought, word, and action in my life.
And may my patience radiate peace and strength to all those around me.
In your name, I pray,
Amen.

Notes - Personal Prayer

A Prayer of Integrity

Divine Creator
I come to you now with a desire to deepen my connection to my integrity.
Provide me with deeper insight into myself so I can improve and live a life of unwavering integrity.
I deeply desire to embrace the qualities of honesty, honor, and moral uprightness.

Remind me in moments of temptation to uphold
the highest ethical standards in all areas of my life,
To let my actions align with my values and principles no matter the situation.

Bless me with the strength to stand for what is right,
Even in the face of challenges, temptations, or popular opinion.
Instill in me a clear ability to discern between right and wrong,
To choose integrity over deceit, and honor over dishonesty.

Help me to be true to myself and authentic in all that I do,
Acting with transparency and accountability.
Remind me with the strength and duty to myself to take responsibility for my actions,
To admit my mistakes and seek amends with acceptance.
Help me build even more into a person of my word,
Fulfilling my commitments and promises with integrity.

Teach me to be a person of compassion that treats others with fairness and respect,
To honor their dignity and embrace their diversity.
Help me to reinforce the trust in my relationships,
And to inspire trust in others through my unwavering integrity.

Support me in my desire to align my thoughts, words, and actions
With integrity and into every aspect of my being.

Remind me to lead by example, and to inspire others to embrace integrity as a way of life.
Divine Creator, I ask for your help in becoming more of a steadfast human
That remains true to my values and in the light no matter the situation.
I seek to live with honor and moral uprightness.

With your support and direction may I live a life with even more
Integrity so its value may influence itself in every thought, word, and action.
May my integrity radiate truth and righteousness to all.
In your name, I pray,
Amen.

Notes - Personal Prayer

A Prayer of Productivity

Divine Creator
I pray now asking for your help in increasing my productivity even more.
Help me focus on living a life of purposeful action.
Remind me to embrace the qualities of focus, discipline, and efficiency.
Grant me opportunities to learn from you through others that have mastered
These qualities.
With your healing hand please assist me in removing unhealthy distractions
That are not aligned with my purpose or life's calling.
Help me identify my priorities and to set clear goals with action.

Remind me to use my time and energy wisely in pursuit of meaningful endeavors.
Reinforce my decision now with motivation and determination to overcome procrastination,
And to embrace a mindset of productivity and achievement.

Give me the clarity to know the difference between tasks that bring true value,
And those that merely distract or drain my energy.
Help me to streamline my efforts and focus on what truly matters,
So that I may make the most of each day and maximize my potential.

Help me improve my ability to manage my time effectively,
To create a balance between work, rest, and rejuvenation.
Support me to set healthy boundaries and honor my personal needs,
So that I may sustain my productivity and well-being in the long run.

Ignite me with even more creativity to find innovative solutions and approaches,
To think outside the box and overcome challenges with resilience.

Help me shift my mindset towards growth and to view failures as lessons and opportunity
to adapt and continuously improve.
Gift me with the ability to collaborate and delegate when needed,
To leverage the strengths and talents of others in achieving shared goals.
Help me create a supportive and productive environment in home and work,
Where teamwork and synergy thrive, and accomplishments are celebrated.

Divine Creator, I express my deepest desire to increase my productivity,
For the ability to channel my energy towards meaningful endeavors.
For your assistance in removing wasteful distractions from my life as I
Seek to remain on my path of purpose.
Thank you for the constant guidance and love you provide in my life,
And for the reminder that through productivity, we fulfill our purpose.

May I take action and with your help inject more productivity into every thought and action in my life.
May my efforts contribute to the betterment of myself and the world.
In your name of purpose, I pray,
Amen

Notes - Personal Prayer

A Prayer of Accomplishment

Divine Creator
I speak to you now seeking help in the matters of accomplishment.
I do not come from a place of lack but from a place of seeking opportunity for more.
Help me embrace the qualities of perseverance, determination, and success.
Remind me to set clear goals and envision the path to achievement.
Support me in turning intention into action with an unshakeable commitment
To see it through to completion.
Reinforce my choices with courage to pursue my dreams and aspirations and
Bless me with the motivation and drive to overcome obstacles.
In moments of doubt, remind me to not lose sight of my purpose in the face of challenges.

Do not allow failures to dissuade my spirit or desire for accomplishment,
Help me see them with a wider lens and as the vehicle for growth and refinement.
Build me with resilience and with the power to bounce back with renewed strength,
Keeping my focus on the ultimate vision of accomplishment.

Allow me the discipline to take consistent action,
To prioritize my tasks and manage my time effectively.
Guide me to make productive choices and use my resources wisely,
So that I may make steady progress toward my desired accomplishments.

Remind me to celebrate small victories along the way,
To acknowledge and appreciate the milestones achieved.
Grant me flexibility and openness to listen to what is required so I can pivot when necessary.
Remind me to find joy and fulfillment in the journey and each day,
Knowing that every step forward is a testament to my commitment.

Bless me with the awareness to recognize and appreciate the contributions of others,
To seek out collaboration and surround myself with a supportive community of talented
Individuals. Teach me to share my accomplishments with thankfulness and generosity,
Inspiring and uplifting others on their own paths of achievement.

Divine Creator, I speak to you in wonder of the example of achievement
You have shown through your creations and ask for your help
to set my own goals and manifest them into reality.
Thank you for the continuous blessings and guidance you provide,
And for the reminder that through accomplishment, we fulfill one part of our potential.

Help me shift my mindset towards being focused on accomplishment and success
While embracing the path and steps towards getting there.
May all my achievements large and small contribute to the betterment of myself and the world.
In your name, I pray,
Amen.

Notes - Personal Prayer

A Prayer of Positivity

Divine Creator
I speak to you now with my heart and hands wide open ready to receive your love.
I ask for your help to create a more positive mindset and to rid me of any
Negative self-talk. I desire to become my own number one fan rather than
My number one critic as it is no longer serving me or helping me advance into
My greatness.
I wish to replace my negativity with qualities of optimism, gratitude and encouragement.
Help me to see the beauty and goodness in all that surrounds me,
To focus on the blessings and possibilities in every situation.

Teach me to shift my perspective from challenges to opportunities,
And to find strength and hope even in the midst of doubt.
Rid me of any victim mentality and equip me with the tool and lessons
From others to learn from.
Remind me to choose uplifting thoughts and words,
To speak words of kindness, and love.

Help me to release any negativity and judgment,
And to radiate positivity in all my interactions.
Remind me with the awareness to nurture my inner peace and well-being,
To prioritize self-care and engage in activities that uplift my spirit.

Urge me to surround myself with positive influences,
And to seek inspiration and wisdom from sources that uplift my soul.
Provide me with strength to tackle obstacles and hardship with resilience,
To believe in my own abilities and the power of positivity.

Remind me to trust in the divine plan and to have faith in the journey;
That my timing and the Creators time are not connected but that
everything happens for a higher purpose with perfect timing.
Remind me to have understanding and to extend positivity to others,
To offer support, encouragement, and love in their times of need;
Motive free.
Ignite me to be an even brighter beacon of light and positivity,
And let my example Inspire others to embrace the transformative power of a positive mindset.

Divine Creator, I desperately desire to be a force of beaming positivity,
To shift my mindset and outlook to being fully in the light.
I wish to radiate pure joy, gratitude, and optimism at all times and if
I stray into negativity to have the quickness to convert back.

May I express positivity in every thought, word, and action,
And may my positivity spread out to touch the lives of all beings.
In your name of light, I pray,
Amen.

Notes - Personal Prayer

A Prayer of Clarity

Divine Creator
I speak to you now asking for help to remove any confusion clouding my mind.
I seek to gain more internal and external clarity so I can take decisive and purposeful action.
I'm not asking for all things to be revealed as I want to embrace the uncertainty of life with
Excitement. I am asking for your help that when there are questions looming
that I can connect to your divine signal and find peace with clarity.

Teach me to embrace the qualities of insight, discernment, and understanding.
Help me to quiet the noise and distractions in my mind,
To create space for clarity to emerge and illuminate my path.

Reinforce my ability to listen to the internal voice of my soul,
And to trust the inner guidance that leads me towards truth.

Grant me the intelligence to ask the right questions,
To seek answers with an open mind and a receptive heart without
A personal attachment to the answer.
Help me to let go of preconceived notions,
And to embrace new perspectives and fresh insights.

Encourage me to face the truth and facts and do not
Let me justify bad behavior of myself or in others,
Even when it may be uncomfortable or challenging.
Help me recognize and release illusions and self-deception,
So that I may see reality with clarity and authenticity.

Remind me of the power of patience to wait for clarity to unfold,
To trust in the divine timing of understanding and revelation.

Free me of my need for immediate answers and instant results
And to embrace the process of exploration and discovery excitement.
Train me with the ability to discern between what is essential and what is not,
To prioritize my time, energy, and focus on what truly matters.

Help me to make decisions from a place of clarity and alignment
And not from fear or lack.

Divine Creator, I speak from love and desire to boost my ability
to see through confusion and find inner truth.
May I develop more clarity by connecting stronger to my divine signal
To you the creator and have the trust and confidence to hear it.
May my clarity of purpose inspire and uplift those around me.
In your name of wisdom, I pray,
Amen.

Notes - Personal Prayer

A Prayer of Rest

Divine Creator
I pray to you now asking for your support in balancing work and rest.
At times I have trouble turning off my brain and setting time aside for rest
feels uncomfortable. Please Grant me the guidance
to find and schedule deep and rejuvenating rest.

Help me train my mind towards being able to embrace
the qualities of stillness, tranquility, and restoration.
Teach me to release the burdens and worries that weigh me down
To remind me that rest is an essential part of balance and productivity.
Help me better develop my ability to quiet my mind and ease my soul,

Allow me the insight and trust to listen to the signals from my body,
So I can honor its need for rest and replenishment.
Help me to design healthy boundaries and prioritize self-care,
So that I may nurture my physical, emotional, and spiritual well-being.

Show me how peace surpasses all understanding,
That even in the midst of chaos and busyness, I may find calm.
Guide me to find solace in the simplicity of the present moment,
And to savor the quiet moments of rest that nourish my body and soul.

Encourage me to let go of the need for constant productivity,
To recognize the value of rest as an essential element of any journey.

I seek to live a life that is harmonious and sustainable and ask for
Your support in designing that better.,
Help me awaken each day with renewed energy and vitality.
Teach me how to create a sanctuary of rest in my surroundings and within myself
So I can retreat and find peace in your loving presence.
Remind me to pause when I feel overwhelmed, help me dis-engage and detach
So I can better re-engage with fresh insight and energy.

Divine Creator, I ask you show me the importance of rest
And help me design a structure that is balanced between
Work and time to recharge.May my restfulness radiate peace and serenity to all
And lead me on a path of becoming my better self.
In your name, I pray,
Amen

Notes - Personal Prayer

A Prayer for Energy

Divine Creator
I speak to you now feeling a bit tired seeking your help to find renewed vitality.
Please provide me with your guidance to access and channel abundant energy.
Help me to develop more evolved qualities of strength, vitality, and enthusiasm.
Teach me to connect with the wellspring of energy that flows within me,
To tap into its limitless reserves and unleash its power.

Help me know when it's time to double down and when it's time to pump the brakes to recharge and revitalize my body, mind, and spirit. I never want to be too depleted so I can live each day with vitality and vigor.

Remind me to nourish my physical body with wholesome foods, to feed my mind
With expansive knowledge, and to practice spirituality to refuel my soul.

Help me to prioritize regular exercise and movement,
To invigorate my physical being and release stagnant energy.
Bless me with the clarity and focus to align my actions with my purpose,
To channel my energy into endeavors that bring me joy and fulfillment.

Guide me to let go of energy-draining activities and relationships,
And to create a life that is in harmony with what matters to me.
Support me with the resilience to overcome fatigue and exhaustion,
To bounce back from challenges and setbacks with renewed strength.

Bless me with the inspiration and motivation to pursue my passions,
To engage in activities that ignite my spirit and fuel my creativity.
Provide me with the strength to disconnect from the distractions that
Are no longer serving me; even if it means that I have to step into the unknown.

Guide me to surround myself with positive and uplifting influences,
And to share my energy with others in acts of kindness and love.
Protect me from the energy vampires of the world and allow me to
Swifty identify and disconnect from any such people that surround me.

Divine Creator, help me tap into the infinite energy field, that I may
Be renewed on a cellular level.
Thank you for the continuous blessings and guidance you provide,
With a humble heart and a commitment to developing vibrant energy,
I turn to your divine guidance.
May my radiant energy inspire and uplift those around me.
In your name, I pray,
Amen

Notes - Personal Prayer

A Prayer about the Dream Life

Divine Creator
I speak to you now as work in progress striving to attain a life more inline with my dreams.
Grant me the guidance and blessings to manifest my deepest desires and aspirations.
Help me to create a life that aligns with my purpose, values, and highest potential.
Guide me to envision the elements that compose my dream life and help me set action
Towards building it.

Help me to define what brings me joy, fulfillment, and meaning. Help me focus in on
The kind of life I want to design. Assist me in manifesting a life that encompasses abundance, love, and
purposeful pursuits.

Encourage me to pursue my dreams and to never settle for less than what I have the potential to achieve.
Help me to trust in my abilities, embrace growth opportunities, and learn from challenges.
Reinforce my decision making with positive signals when my choices align with my authentic self and lead me
towards fulfillment.
Help me build my dream life to include harmony, peace, and a deep sense of gratitude.
May it be a life where love, compassion, and kindness flourish abundantly.
Provide me with the necessary lessons and trials that expedite my growth on the path towards my dream life
and assist me in cultivating meaningful relationships, cherished connections, and a supportive community.

Assist me with the supporting resources, opportunities and network to aid in my manifestation of my dream
life and use me as an instrument to help others on their journey of life.
Teach me how to attract abundance in all areas, including health, wealth, and personal growth.
Support me to make choices that contribute to the greater good and make a positive impact.

Divine Creator, may my dream life unfold in ways that exceed my expectations,
And may it be a life filled with purpose, love, and deep fulfillment.
With a grateful heart and unwavering faith,
I trust my dreams to your divine hands.
May my dream life become a reality that inspires and uplifts others,
And may it contribute to the greater good of all.
In your name, I pray,
Amen.

Notes - Personal Prayer

A Prayer about the Dream House

Divine Creator
I come before you with a different request as I have a vision for my dream house I would like
Your assistance in helping bring to fruition.

I need your guidance to create a sacred space that reflects my desires, values, and aspirations.
Guide me to envision the perfect home, filled with love, warmth, and serenity.
Bless me with the clarity and decisiveness to define the features and characteristics that align with my taste and personality.

Assist me in manifesting a home that provides comfort, security, and a sense of belonging.
Provide me with the resources and opportunities to make my dream house a reality.
Help me to navigate the practical aspects of finding, designing, and acquiring the perfect home.

Guide me to make wise life choices and to attract the right people and circumstances to support my vision.
Bless my dream house with love and positive energy and release it from the ether so it can
Come down into reality sooner. May my dream house be a sanctuary that nurtures the physical, emotional, and spiritual well-being of all those who enter it.

Bless me with the ability to create a home that welcomes loved ones and cultivates cherished memories.
Divine Creator, I say thank you for allowing me your gift of envisioning my dream house.
Thank you for the continuous blessings and guidance you provide.

May my dream house become a reality that exceeds my expectations,
And may it be a place where love, joy, and peace flourish.

With a grateful heart and unwavering faith,
I surrender my dream to your divine guidance and wisdom.
May my dream house be a reflection of my truest self,
And may it serve as a haven of happiness and fulfillment.
In your name, I pray,
Amen.

Notes - Personal Prayer

A Prayer of Action

Divine Creator
I come before you with a heart filled with intention and a deep desire
to turn my aspirations into reality. Grant me the wisdom, courage, and perseverance
to implement my intentions into meaningful action.
Help me to align my thoughts, words, and deeds with the vision I hold in my heart.

Guide me to set clear and specific goals that reflect my truest desires and purpose.
Bless me with the clarity to identify the necessary steps
and resources needed to bring my intentions to life.

Assist me in creating a plan of action that is both practical and aligned
with my soul's calling.
Grant me the strength and determination to overcome any obstacles or doubts that may arise along the way.
Help me to navigate challenges with resilience,
knowing that they are opportunities for growth and learning.
Fill my heart with unwavering faith and trust in the process of manifestation.

Bless me with the motivation and discipline to take consistent action towards my goals.
Guide me to prioritize my time, energy, and resources
in ways that support the realization of my intentions.
Help me to stay focused and committed, even when faced with distractions or setbacks.

Divine Creator, I express my gratitude for the gift of intention
and the power to bring dreams into reality.
Thank you for the continuous blessings and guidance you provide.
May I be a co-creator with you, aligning my will with your divine plan.

With a humble heart and unwavering determination,
I surrender to your wisdom and guidance.
May my intentions be brought to life in ways that serve the highest good of all.
May my actions be filled with love, purpose, and positive impact.
In your name of divine manifestation, I pray,
Amen.

Notes - Personal Prayer

A Prayer of Transformation

Divine Creator
I come before you now having reached my limit of my current self asking for a release.
Grant me the strength, clarity, and guidance to remove negativity from my life.
Help me to create a space of peace, positivity, and harmony within and around me.

Guide me to recognize and acknowledge the sources of negativity in my life and
bless me with the discernment to identify negative thought patterns, toxic relationships, and draining environments.
Assist me in releasing any attachments to negativity and in
finding healthier and more uplifting alternative sources of fuel.

Help me to replace negative thoughts with positive affirmations and self-belief.
Teach me to grow into a mindset of gratitude, compassion, and forgiveness, both towards myself and others.
Bless me with the strength to set clear boundaries and protect my energy.
Help me to surround myself with supportive and loving individuals who uplift and inspire me.
Push me to engage in activities that bring happiness, light-heartedness and fulfillment.

Divine Creator, I trust in your power to remove negativity from my life.
Thank you for allowing me endless opportunities to grow .
May I be a channel of love and light, radiating positivity and strength into the world.

With a heart ready for change and a commitment to transformation, I trust in your divine guidance.
May negativity be dissolved, replaced by positivity and love.
May I walk the path of light, free from the shadows of negativity.
In your name of infinite love, I pray,
Amen.

Notes - Personal Prayer

A Prayer of Protection

Divine Creator
I pray to you with a sincere request for your divine protection.
Can you please shield me from danger, both seen and unseen,
and keep me safe in all aspects of my life.
Surround me with your loving presence and guide me away from harm's way.

Give me the awareness to recognize potential dangers and make wise choices.
Help me to navigate through life with caution and intuition.
Illuminate the path before me, so I may avoid obstacles and harmful situations.
Protect me from physical harm, accidents, and illness.
Safeguard my well-being and that of my loved ones.
Create a shield of divine light around me,
deflecting any negative energies or intentions directed towards me.

Guard my mind and emotions from the destructive forces of fear, anxiety, and negativity.
Strengthen my inner resolve and grant me the courage
to face challenges with grace and resilience.
Help me to trust in your divine protection,
knowing that I am always held in your loving embrace.

Divine Protector, I want to say thank you from my depths of my soul
for the continuous protection you provide.
May your divine presence be my fortress,
and may your love and light surround me at all times.

With unwavering faith and trust in your divine protection,
I release my fears and worries to your care.
May I walk in the knowledge that I am safe and secure under your watchful eye.
In your name of infinite protection, I pray,
Amen.

Notes - Personal Prayer

A Prayer of Focus

Divine Creator
I come before you seeking your assistance in finding focus amidst the distractions of life.
Grant me the strength, discipline, and acuity of mind
to stay focused on my goals and aspirations.
Help me to direct my energy and attention towards that which truly matters.

Guide me to identify my priorities and align them with my purpose and values.
Bless me with the ability to decide between
what is essential and what is merely a distraction.
Assist me in letting go of the unnecessary and
staying committed to the path that leads to my highest self.

Grant me the resilience to overcome any challenge that may divert my focus.
Help me to stay steadfast in the face of temptation or self-doubt.
Fill me with unwavering determination to pursue my dreams
with laser focus and dedication.

Bless my mind with clarity and sharpness.
Clear away any mental clutter or fog that hinders my ability to concentrate.
Help me to cultivate a calm and centered state of mind, free from worry and scattered thoughts.

Divine Creator, I express my gratitude for your help in sharpening my focus
and the ability to channel my energy towards what truly matters.
Thank you for always listening and providing me with endless opportunities to improve.
May I walk my path of growth with focus, staying true to my purpose
and making a meaningful impact.
May my focus be unwavering,
and may my actions be purposeful and aligned with my soul's calling.
In your name, I pray,
Amen.

Notes - Personal Prayer

A Prayer to Mother Earth

Divine Creator
I speak to you with thanks and love with a deep reverence and gratitude
For the wonders of nature that surround me. I also say thank you
For the gift of having a deep connection and involvement with nature.

Help me to further recognize and honor the beauty, wisdom, and sacredness of all living beings and the earth itself.
Encourage me to immerse myself in the healing power of nature.
Bless me with the awareness to appreciate the intricate ecosystems,
the diversity of species, and the harmony that exists in the natural world.
Assist me in my support for stewardship for our planet.

Teach me to slow down and be fully present in nature's embrace.
Help me to listen to the whispers of the wind, the rustling of leaves, and the songs of birds.
Open my senses to the sights, sounds, scents, and textures
that awakens a sense of awe and wonder within me.
Allow me to connect with nature daily and
to always remember your creations are superior to all.
Guide me to live in harmony with nature and
to honor the delicate balance of the earth.
Inspire me to make choices
that promote sustainability, conservation, and the well-being of all living beings.

Divine Creator, I express my deep love and gratitude
for the abundance and beauty of the natural world.
Thank you for nature's teachings.
May I continue to have more opportunities to learn from Mother Nature
and connect to my primal self.
May I become a caretaker and advocate for the earth,
protecting and nurturing its precious resources.

With a loving heart and a desire to reconnect with nature's wisdom,
I release control and only ask for your guidance and wisdom.
May my connection with nature deepen,
allowing me to experience the interconnectedness of all life
and to walk in harmony with the natural rhythms of the earth.
In your name of divine connection and reverence for nature, I pray,
Amen.

Notes - Personal Prayer

A Prayer of Spirituality

Divine Creator
I come before you with a yearning to nurture my spirituality
and deepen my connection with the sacred.
Grant me the guidance, insight, and devotion to create a rich and fulfilling spiritual practice.
Help me to align my heart, mind, and soul with the divine presence
that resides within and around me.

Guide me to seek truth and meaning in my spiritual journey.
Bless me with the curiosity to explore various paths and teachings,
embracing what resonates with my soul and ignites my inner flame.
Encourage me in finding moments of stillness and silence
to listen to the voices of my spirit
and the gentle guidance of your divine presence.

Give me the ability to open my heart to the beauty and wonder
of the universe and to recognize the sacredness in everyday moments,
the interconnectedness of all beings, and the divine spark within each soul.
May my spirituality be grounded in love, compassion, and service to others.

Bestow upon me the strength
to overcome doubts on my spiritual path.
Fill me with faith and trust in the unfolding of my journey,
even in times of uncertainty.
Encourage me to let go of limiting thoughts
and embrace the expansiveness of spiritual growth.

Divine Creator, I express my love for the ability to practice spirituality
and the opportunity to connect with the sacred.
There are no words to describe my gratitude for the guidance you provide.
May my spirituality be a source of comfort, inspiration, and transformation in my life.

With a humble heart and a deep yearning for spiritual growth,
I trust in your divine judgment.
May my spiritual practice nourish my soul, align me with divine truth,
and bring me closer to the essence of who I am.
In your name of infinite love, I pray,
Amen.

Notes - Personal Prayer

A Prayer of Potential

Divine Creator
I come before you with a deep desire to unlock and fulfill my true potential.
Guide me on this journey of self-discovery and growth,
helping me to recognize and embrace
the unique gifts and talents you have bestowed upon me.

Grant me the clarity to envision the highest expression
of myself and the courage to pursue it wholeheartedly.
Remove any self-doubt or limiting beliefs that hold me back from stepping into my full potential.
Fill me with confidence,
knowing that I am supported by your infinite wisdom and love.

Assist me in identifying and cultivating the skills
and abilities that align with my purpose.
Inspire me to continually learn, grow, and refine my talents.
Show me the path that leads to the realization
of my dreams and aspirations,
empowering me to overcome obstacles
with resilience and determination.

Help me to recognize the opportunities
that arise along my journey, and to seize them with enthusiasm and gratitude.
May each experience be a stepping stone towards reaching my highest potential,
and may I embrace both successes and failures as valuable lessons for growth.

Divine Creator, I express my deep gratitude for the unique gifts
and potential that lies within me.
Thank you for the support you provide as I strive to achieve my highest purpose.
May I walk the path of self-discovery with humility, integrity,
and a deep reverence for the possibilities that await.

With an open heart and a commitment to growth,
I ask for the strength and resilience to embrace my true potential and
to make a meaningful impact in the world.
In your name, I pray,
Amen.

Notes - Personal Prayer

A Prayer for Recovering from Illness

Divine Creator
I come before you with a fervent prayer,
seeking your divine intervention and help in overcoming illness.

I release my fears, worries, and doubts,
placing my trust in your infinite power.
Grant me the strength and resilience to face this illness
with courage and determination.

Strengthen my body, mind, and spirit, empowering me to endure the challenges that lie ahead.
Fill me with hope, knowing that your healing touch can bring restoration and wellness.
Guide the hands of the healthcare professionals who are providing me with care and treatment.
Grant them the correct protocol, skill, and compassion as they work tirelessly to restore my health.
May their efforts be guided by your divine leadership
and may they be the instruments of your healing grace.

Surround me with a loving support system,
including family, friends, and loved ones, who offer encouragement, comfort, and prayers.
Grant them the patience and strength to uplift me during this difficult time,
and may their love and presence be a source of solace and healing.

Divine Creator, I express my gratitude for the precious gift of life and ask in this time of trial you lift
All stress and negativity so my body and mind can align onto the healing frequency.
Guide me to eat healing foods, to drink healing liquids and follow your direction
So I can restore my well-being.

With an unwavering faith and trust in your divine will, I place my healing journey in your hands. May your
healing power flow through me, restoring me to health, vitality, and wholeness.
In your name, I pray,
Amen.

Notes - Personal Prayer

A Prayer for Friendship

Divine Creator
I come before you with a heartfelt desire to welcome new friendships into my life.
Guide me on this journey of building meaningful connections with others,
that I may find companionship, understanding, and support.

Open my heart and mind to the opportunities that exist for new friendships to blossom.
Help me to recognize the kindred spirits who cross my path,
and grant me the courage to reach out and initiate meaningful interactions.
Grant me the wisdom to listen attentively, to truly see and understand others.

May I offer genuine compassion, empathy, and acceptance to those I encounter, nurturing the seeds of
friendship and creating a safe space for connection to grow.

Divine Creator, most of all I would like your help to attract new friends to have
shared laughter, shared experiences, and shared moments of growth. May these new friendships enrich my
life and bring joy, support, and companionship.

With an open heart and a genuine desire to connect I say thank you for listening.
May the friendships I cultivate be authentic, nurturing, and built upon a foundation of mutual respect and
understanding.
In your name of infinite connection, I pray,
Amen.

Notes - Personal Prayer

A Prayer of Thanks

Divine Creator
With a heart overflowing with gratitude,
I pray to you to offer my deepest thanks and appreciation for the abundant gifts in my life.
You have bestowed upon me countless blessings, both seen and unseen,
and I am humbled by your unwavering love and grace.

I am grateful for the gift of life itself
and for the endless variety of experience provided throughout the journey of it.
Thank you for the precious moments, the joys, and the challenges
that have shaped me into who I am today.
Each experience has been a teacher, guiding me towards growth and wisdom.
I express my deep love for the beauty of nature that surrounds me,
the vibrant colors, the fragrant scents, and the melodies of birds.
Thank you for the sun that warms my skin and the earth that supports my every step.
Your creation is a constant reminder of your infinite creativity and love.

I am thankful for the gift of relationships
the cherished bonds with family, friends, and loved ones.
Thank you for the support, laughter, and companionship they bring into my life.
May our connections continue to deepen and be a source of happiness and strength.

I say thank you for the abundance that fills my life
the provision of food, shelter, and all my needs.
Thank you for the endless opportunities that come my way,
for the talents and abilities with which I have been blessed.
May I use these gifts to make a positive difference in the lives of others.

Divine Creator, I am eternally grateful for your presence in my life
the gentle guidance, the whispers of intuition, and the unconditional love that envelops me.
Thank you for your unwavering support and for walking beside me
in every step of my journey.
With a heart brimming with gratitude,
I offer my thanks for all the blessings, big and small.
May my gratitude be a continuous prayer, an expression of my love and
appreciation for all that you have provided.
In your name of infinite love, I pray,
Amen.

Notes - Personal Prayer

Made in the USA
Columbia, SC
08 January 2024